Mobile!

City by the Bay

edited by Cathy Patrick

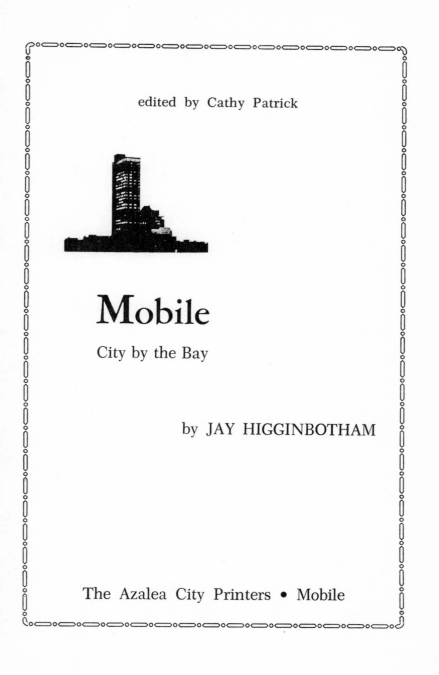

Mobile

City by the Bay

by JAY HIGGINBOTHAM

The Azalea City Printers • Mobile

Books by JAY HIGGINBOTHAM

The Mobile Indians

Family Biographies

The Pascagoula Indians

Pascagoula—Singing River City

Mobile!—City by the Bay

FIRST EDITION

Library of Congress Catalog Card Number 68-58255

Printed in the United States of America
by The Azalea City Printers
Mobile, Ala.

To Uncle Barney
and Aunt Gladys

THE REVEREND AND MRS. M. S. VARNADO

Contents

Acknowledgments

Introduction

CHAPTER

Acknowledgements

Without the help of the following individuals, this book would not have been easily written. Despite the accessibility of a wealth of organized material regarding the first two centuries of Mobile's history, the same can not be said of subject matter concerning the present century.

For assistance in helping to penetrate the maze of unorganized court records, newspaper files and family archives pertaining to this neglected period of Mobile's past, I am indebted to Ruth Warren, Caldwell Delaney, Harry Seale, Bart Chamberlain Jr., Robert Donovan, John Mandeville, J. Oliver Wintzell, Townsend Ellis, Joe Hendrix, Bishop W. T. Phillips, Mrs. Charles Cason, Bill Hearin, H. D. Hudson, Sam Johnston, Bobby Jackson, Frank Pryor, Mike Blake, Robert Smith, J. E. Drain, Tom Ford, Gwen Napper, Glenda Shelly, Mrs. David Patton, Miss Alice Frazer, E. Herndon Smith, Miss Emma Harris, Mr. Charles Rheme, Mr. Jim Mann, Mr. Tyler Turner, Mr. Frank Brown, Mr. Richard Turner, Mobile Press Register, Mr. Emory Arnette, Mr. Dana Cessna.

I wish to thank Mr. Dewey Freeman for lending me the Freeman House to do the actual writing.

Most of all, I wish to thank the editor, Miss Cathy Patrick, who did much of the research and typing, collected the pictures, designed the jacket and assumed responsibility for the production of the book.

August 1968
Mobile, Alabama

JAY HIGGINBOTHAM

Introduction

The dawn gently breaks and the rising sun peeks over the trees of Baldwin County, over the tranquil waters of Mobile Bay and strikes a strange, new object pointing headlong into the sky. The First National Bank glistens at its crest, austerely dominating the skyline. An old fisherman with a cane pole and a slouch hat, perched on the causeway, watches the shadow slowly fall down the building.

The light is broken into myriad rays, some of which settle through the trees of Bienville Square and focus on a yawning squirrel. He scampers down the trunk of an old oak tree and skips across the grass, across the sidewalk and underneath an iron-laced bench where a bearded man sleeps, the green edition of last evening's Mobile Press spread over his shoulders. The squirrel picks up a peanut and listens intently at the snoring overhead. The sleeping man moves his foot and the squirrel's ears quicken. He dashes over to the circular pool and hops onto the concrete siding, listening to the cascade of water dropping into the pool. He picks at the peanut and a particle of shell falls into the water. A sleek, orange goldfish slides up to kiss it at the surface.

At the far corner of the square, a group of pigeons suddenly flap their wings when the air is pierced by the clanging of an iron bin.

"Got it, Sam!" a voice echoes through the hollows between the buildings. "Move it out!" And the garbage truck rumbles down St. Francis Street. It turns at the corner of Claiborne Street and one of the garbage men flips a cigarette butt at the lions guarding entrance to the Scottish Rite Temple. "The cat's got the hot foot," he snickers to himself and wipes his mouth on his sleeve.

The driver stops at the corner, looks to his right and sees a taxi rolling up Dauphin Street. The taxi passes a large, columned building and the man in the back seat gapes out the window.

"What kind of church is that?" he asks.

"That's the Basilica," answers the cab driver. "Basilica of the Immaculate Conception. They got a organ in there that'll rattle your sacroilliac."

The sun rises higher in the sky and Mobile Bay glitters in the growing light of day. A cool Gulf breeze is blowing out of the southeast. A young man in a green Mustang crosses a bridge on the highway east of the city and nearly runs off the road when he sees a huge battleship about to ram the causeway. He blinks, shakes his head, then gets back on the road and drives to the Bankhead Tunnel.

Across town, the seven o'clock bus is crossing the tracks at the Loop and heading up Government Street. It stops at the Houston Street intersection and two baggy-eyed passengers step on. In the routine pace of a busy metropolitan transporter, the bus moves its work-bound load up the oak-lined street, oblivious to a beauty the passengers have come to take for granted. They pass the rows of old mansions and azaleas without comment. The First Baptist Church, the Public Library, the Raphael Semmes home and the old Barton Academy all sail by the window unnoticed. Then the Municipal Auditorium and the Spanish Plaza come into view and the riders perk up. A few of them step off the bus at the next stop and cross the street toward the *Mobile Press Register* building.

Passing the Admiral Semmes Hotel, the bus moves on, stopping for a red light, then bypasses the Bankhead Tunnel entrance near the Court House. Taking a sharp left at the Royal Street corner near the spot where Octavia Le Vert once entertained the world-famous, the bus rounds the turn and heads up Royal Street into the thickening traffic. Stopping in front of Hammel's Department Store, the driver deposits seven of his passengers. Then moving to the famed Battle House Hotel, the bus stops again and the remaining passengers stream from the doors and melt into the expanding crowds. Mobile has awakened and its people go forth to meet the new day!

There is a wave of optimism flooding Mobile today but it has not always been so. Over the years, no city in America has borne more heavily the disasters of floods, fires, invading armies, hurricanes, Indian attacks and yellow fever epidemics as has Mobile, Alabama. Founded in 1702 by Jean-Baptiste Le Moyne, Sieur de Bienville, the town has slowly but steadily grown into a bustling city of a quarter-million inhabitants.

The turning point in Mobile's economic surge was the dredging of the channel from the mouth of the Mobile River to the Gulf. Congress authorized the project in

1888 and Mobilians soon had themselves a 280-foot-wide channel with a central depth of twenty-three feet. Since the dredging project, Mobile's enduring position as a port has been assured. The port is supported, too, by a wealth of industries. The International Paper Mill and Scott Paper Mill both send an avalanche of acrid fumes to settle on the vast Mobile Delta. Mobile Pulley and Machine Works is one of the South's largest foundries. Waterman Steamship Company is reputed to be one of the world's largest. And, of course, the many shipyards, big and small, that surround the bay, are constantly producing vessels, from sailboats to ocean liners.

But it is not so much industry and commerce that the true Mobilian takes pride in describing to the tourist. The native son or daughter would rather boast of the things which set the port city off from other American cities. He would rather tell about the world-renowned Bellingrath Gardens or the gay carnival season of Mardi Gras when the whole city becomes alive in a grand display of color and frivolity. He might speak of the Deep Sea Fishing Rodeo at Dauphin Island and the sailboat races around Mobile Bay. Or the delectable Créole dishes and sea foods that abound in the city's many fine restaurants.

Then, of course, the native likes to talk about football, about the annual Senior Bowl game which brings together more all-stars than any of America's other bowl games. He might also point out the campus of Spring Hill College and the grounds of Mobile College and the rapidly expanding University of South Alabama.

If there were time, he would like to take the tourist up in a Piper Cub for a spin around the bay and point out some amazing sights. The magnificence of the giant battleship, U.S.S. Alabama, is startling enough but a few miles to the northeast is a much more spectacular sight, a veritable graveyard of convoy vessels, Liberty and

Victory ships that have been mothballed since World War II. As many as 350 of them have been stored away at one time, awaiting the day when again they may be recalled to service in some future war. Then a few miles to the northwest, a giant Indian mound rises out of the wildernesses of the Mobile Delta, a timeless monument of the Mobile Indians who, centuries ago, piled the dirt in tribute to their gods and for their own personal welfare.

However, what Mobilians take most pride in is the abundance of beauty, charm and grace. The Azalea Trail and Bellingrath Gardens are well known. And it doesn't take the visitor long to grasp the beauty of Spanish moss hanging from the majestic old oak trees. But *"Les belles Mobiliens"* must certainly be God's finest handiwork. The Southern Belle is awe-inspiring in literature and history and in Mobile she reaches her apex. During ante-bellum days, the wealthy southern planter, Sam Houston among others, always made at least one trip to Mobile in search of the perfect lady. Now thousands come annually to witness the Azalea Trail and Junior Miss pageantry which put on display the South's and the nation's loveliest.

Today, Mobile is known far and wide as the "charm spot of the Deep South." How it developed a reputation for beauty, romance, mystery and charm, is a compelling story, fraught with struggle and sacrifice. It all began many centuries ago, when the land was green and the bay was still.

Chapter 1

Tuskaloosa and DeSoto

Prince Madoc of Wales, so goes the legend, set his sails one bright day in the year 1170 and crossed the Atlantic Ocean. Nearing the mainland of North America, he was caught in a storm and blown past the West Indies and into the Gulf of Mexico.

Sailing to the north, the young Prince drifted into Mobile Bay and found the land fertile and scenic. He then sailed back to Wales and the following year returned with ten shiploads of colonists. After a year or so on the Gulf, Madoc took up his burden and headed north in search of a cooler climate. Marching up through central Alabama, he and his Welshmen made their way to Sand Island on the Ohio River, building stone houses and mating with the Indians along the way. At the falls of the Ohio, Prince Madoc established another colony which later was attacked by the Indians and decimated, but not before a certain amount of blood-mixing took place. The result was a new race of "White Indians" who spoke Welsh and who had an affinity for stone edifices.

Moving to the West, they later became known as the Mandans and perished, to a man, in the year 1836 from smallpox.

The "White Indians" were certainly real enough and Prince Madoc was an historical figure. In the sixteenth century, Richard Hakluyt, the noted British historian and geographer, first brought the story of Prince Madoc's Gulf colony to the world's attention. But it remained for the twentieth century Alabamian, Hatchett Chandler, to tell the world that Madoc's true landing-place was at Fort Morgan at the entrance of Mobile Bay. Skeptics still snicker at Hatchett's claims. Nevertheless, a dugout canoe was recently found in the Mobile Delta that some notable authorities have said is of English origin and dates from the twelfth century.

A few centuries later, in 1497, Amerigo Vespucci was thought to have mapped Mobile Bay. If not true, somebody else must have charted it for the bay shows up very clearly on the Waldsmueller Map of 1507.

In 1519, Alonzo Alvarez de Piñeda coasted past Dauphin Island and up the Mobile River. Ascending the river six leagues, Piñeda saw Indian villages right and left. He was kindly received by the savages and, after trading a trinket or two, came back down river to the present site of Mobile and stayed for forty days. When he had careened his vessels, he pulled anchor and sailed back into the Gulf.

Not until 1528 were the sands of Dauphin Island disturbed again by European invasion. In that year Panfilo de Narvaez and his small fleet hit the Florida coast. Narvaez sighted an Indian village near Pensacola Bay. The savages attacked Narvaez and drove him toward the Bay of Mobile where, three days later, he was again confronted by Indians. At this point, Narvaez was running short of water. A Christian Greek named Doroteo Teodoro and a Negro waded ashore and went to the Indians for something to drink. But they never came back and Narvaez sailed to the West where he was lost at sea near Galveston Island. Twelve years later, Hernando De Soto learned upon arriving in the vicinity that Teodoro and his African companion had been killed at the Indian village of Piachi. As proof of this, DeSoto was shown the dagger that the Greek had brought with him.

In late August of 1540, the DeSoto expedition was resting at the village of Talisi when it received an invitation from Tuskaloosa, chief of the Mobile Indians, to visit him in the nearby town of Athahatchi. A short time later, the Spaniards arrived to accept the invitation. Tuskaloosa received his visitors with all of the pomp and arrogance of a European king. He was seated in a wooden chair with several attendants surrounding him. One of them was fanning him with a large, fly fan made of palmetto. His head was covered with a magnificent headdress. But what had the Spaniards gaping was the tremendous size of the American king. He appeared to be a giant, and his limbs and face were in proportion to the height of his body. He wore a look of severity which well revealed his ferocity and grandeur of spirit.

When DeSoto charged into the plaza where Tuskaloosa sat, he had dismounted his horse and haughtily stepped up to face him. But Tuskaloosa eyed the Spaniard with some aloofness. He made no movement to rise. Then DeSoto, in a daring gesture, grabbed Tuskaloosa by the hand and they went together to seat themselves on the bench that was in the piazza.

"Our men demand women for companionship," DeSoto told Tuskaloosa, "and servants for carrying burdens."

Tuskaloosa replied that he was not accustomed to serving others but rather that it was for others to serve him. But seeing himself surrounded by armed soldiers, Tuskaloosa suggested that DeSoto accompany him to the chief village of Mobila where all these requests would be supplied.

And so they set out for the great town, Tuskaloosa draped over a European horse with his long legs dragging the ground. They crossed the river at Piachi and Monday, October 18, 1540, St. Luke's Day, the curious caravan came to the ancient town of Mobila, somewhere near the Bay of Mobile.

Mobila was strongly fortified, surrounded by great walls and situated on a beautiful plain. Inside the walls were large, wooden cabins full of concealed Indians. Once inside the walls, Tuskaloosa retired to one of the buildings while DeSoto and his small band of men were left in the piazza to wonder as the army encamped outside of town.

DeSoto's fears were somewhat assuaged when Tuskaloosa returned and ordered his dancing girls to perform, after which he said a feast would be held. During the performance, DeSoto noticed some of the savages slyly putting bundles of bows and arrows among the leaves. When Tuskaloosa left the scene to go back into the main cabin, DeSoto became alarmed. He rose to attention as a few stray arrows sailed into the arena. The uneasiness of the savages caused DeSoto to order one of his chief lieutenants, Baltasar de Gallegos, to recall Tuskaloosa from his cabin to quieten his subjects.

Gallegos advanced toward the cabin and DeSoto noticed the Indians standing guard over the entrance to the city. Gallegos was stopped at the door but then forced his way into the cabin. Another of DeSoto's officers, Luis de Moscoso, walked to the entrance of the cabin when Gallegos did not return. The tension was beginning to mount as Moscoso cried out, "Señor Gallegos, come out immediately for we can wait for you no longer!"

Presently, Gallegos returned. On the outside he was challenged by one of Tuskaloosa's sons, a tall, brazen savage. Gallegos drew his sword and disabled the arm of the savage with one fell swoop. The fateful blow had been struck!

Surrounded from all sides, the Spaniards leaped for their horses and fought their way toward the gate. One of the Christians fell dead, an arrow piercing his spine. But DeSoto and the rest of his men bore down on the savages at the gate, slashing them with their long swords and trampling them with their horses. DeSoto took an arrow in his posterior, but the savages, terrified of the horses, abandoned the gate and the Spaniards escaped.

Straggling back to the Spanish camp, DeSoto now had to make a momentous decision. Should he take up his tents and press on to the Gulf or should he return to Mobila to give the wily savages a taste of Christian fortitude?

It took only a moment to decide. No Spaniard of Don Quixote's era would place wisdom above honor. Least of all, the great Castillian Hernando DeSoto. Back to the walls of Mobila rode the six hundred, their banners of the Lord waving in the wind. But the Mobilians were ready for them. They opened the gates and charged the horsemen, seeking to entice the Spaniards to enter the city. Now it was the Spaniards' turn to be cunning. Retreating just enough to lure the Mobilians into the open, they turned on their pursuers and slaughtered them like cattle. Then, taking the dare, the full force of the Castillians charged past the main gate and into the heart of the city. Immediately they were attacked from all sides by more savages than they thought existed and a terrible hand to hand combat ensued. The savages, men, women, and children, attacked the Spaniards with spears, hatchets and rocks. And from the roof tops came flocks of firetipped arrows which settled on the just and unjust alike.

In the heat of the battle DeSoto sounded the call to retreat and the Spaniards retired to a nearby pond to refresh themselves. After a while they again took up their lances and charged back into the city. Desperately the Indians attempted to defend Mobila. Now the entire town was aflame and the savages rushed wildly, almost suicidally, at their oppressors. They even charged the horses that they had so greatly feared at the beginning of the battle. But sticks and stones were no match for Spanish armor. Most of the blows were easily warded off. Now and then a perfectly placed arrow would strike a Christian in the eye or the mouth and he would topple off his steed.

Hour after hour, the battle raged on. Then gradually the Mobilian resistance began to dwindle. Most of the defenders now lay motionless on the battleground while some escaped into the forests.

As dusk settled on the burning town, the harsh sounds of battle diminished to an eerie cacophony of groans and whimpers. The Spanish retreated to the plains and what the historian Bancroft has called "the greatest Indian battle ever fought" was over. Mobila lay in ashes.

The next day DeSoto took a dreadful inventory. He counted twenty dead but this was almost superfluous when compared to his other losses. Nearly every Christian had been wounded, many critically. DeSoto, him-

self, was wounded in such a way that for the next
thirty days he felt more disposed to walking than to riding. To top the climax, the bulk of the army's provisions
was lost in the fire, including two hundred pounds of
pearls with which DeSoto had hoped to entice more
men to his settlement at Mobile Bay and more support
from the Spanish crown. The original plan had been for
DeSoto to traverse the land of Florida in search of
riches so that when he made a rendezvous with Malto-
nado at Mobile Bay, he would have enough gold to found
a great colony. Now he must meet his compatriots
empty-handed.

Fearing mutiny from his men, DeSoto now made the
second of his ill-fated decisions. He must turn around
and march back into the wilderness until he found
enough riches to salvage his pride and his enterprise.
Reluctantly, his disgruntled men followed him to the
north to a rendezvous with destiny and death.

Mobila was left behind in ruins. Once a splendid
town, it had been the citadel of a tribe whose domain
included most of the southern United States. As for
Tuskaloosa, no one ever knew his fate. After the holo-
caust, DeSoto had sought his bones for a prize but the
great chief must have escaped into the forests to help
save the Mobilians from extinction. If the tribe was
nearly decimated, the same was not true for the language. For the Mobile Trade Language became the
"lingua franca" of all the southern Indians and remained
in use all through the French Colonial period.

Two decades after DeSoto, another Spaniard set his
sights on Mobile Bay. Don Tristan De Luna landed somewhere near the bay with 1,500 colonists in 1559. After
settling his colony on the coast, De Luna sent an expedition of two hundred men to explore the interior. After

a journey of forty leagues, they came to the Alabama River and founded a town called Nanipicana that the Indians told them had been burned by white men years earlier.

Once in Nanipicana, De Luna moved all the remaining colonists from the port to that village. When spring came, a scarcity of food forced De Luna to send a party to the Indian village of Coosa. After three months the party returned to Nanipicana and found in a pot buried under a tree a message saying that De Luna had abandoned Nanipicana for lack of food and resources. He had returned to the coast in the spring of 1561 and there the colonists disbanded and returned to Spain. Tristan de Luna had discovered first-hand what his other Spanish brethren had found before him, that the wilderness of Mobile Bay was a prize as elusive as it was beautiful.

Chapter 2

The French Found Mobile

In 1679, a French frigate was attacked and captured by Spanish warships on the Gulf of Mexico. Louis XIV, the grand Monarch of France, immediately ordered three ships to be built to protect French commerce. Informed by his commander in the West Indies of the vulnerability of Havana and Cartegeña, King Louis' ambitions took on a new twist. If he could capture these cities, the remaining Spanish Colonies in the Gulf area would be forced to surrender to France, the ultimate result being the conquest of New Spain.

And so Robert de la Salle was sent down the Mississippi to find a port suitable for harboring ships. But La Salle had other ideas. He wanted to found a colony. After his initial adventure down the great river, La Salle hoodwinked the King into financing a new expedition to establish a fort on the Gulf. He was able to gain Louis' support by convincing him that the Rio Grande, where the King's eyes were set, and the Mississippi were one and the same river! But La Salle's dream was ended with his murder in 1687, after a fiasco which he, himself, promoted by a long chain of deceptions.

Ten years later, the Peace of Ryswick ended the war of the Augsburg League. Spanish fears were thus aroused when it was realized that this treaty now gave Louis XIV some pretext for renewing his designs on the Gulf. Quickly, the Spanish ordered the Viceroy of Mexico to occupy Pensacola Bay. Almost as quickly, the French sent out an expedition under command of Pierre Le Moyne, Sieur d'Iberville. The race for the Gulf was on!

The news had long been out that the best harbor in all the world was Pensacola Bay, a deep, natural port where it was supposed a great river emptied into the Gulf. Accordingly, Iberville set his sights on Pensacola and after a stormy voyage across the Atlantic dropped his anchors in the outer harbor on January 26, 1699. To his dismay, Iberville found himself staring at a Spanish flag waving arrogantly over a puny little fort. However, seeing that no great river flowed into that bay, he pulled his anchors and sailed further west. After excursions on Dauphin and Horn Islands, he anchored his big vessels at Ship Island and switched to long boats and canoes in search of a suitable harbor. Rediscovering the Mississippi River, he ascended it for some distance but never found a site to build. He finally decided on the eastern shore of the Bay of Biloxi where he established Fort Maurepas, the first capital of the Louisiana Territory.

Fort Maurepas served as the capital for two years until Iberville could find a spot for a permanent colony. In the meantime, he sent Monsieur Sauvole, his second in command, and his brother, the young Bienville, on scouting expeditions to determine the most strategic location. Bienville found a site on the great river where

New Orleans now stands but it was thought to be too marshy. He searched up and down the coast but the site he finally settled on was a long, high expanse of land on the Mobile River known today as Twenty-Seven Mile Bluff. It was a pleasing site, no doubt, and one which commanded a long view of the river in both directions. Back from the steep bluff was a rich, flat plain, ideal for cultivating, and a small creek that emptied into the river. Five leagues up-river lived the Mobile Indians, a pitiful remnant whose ancestors had almost been destroyed by DeSoto. They had been known to the French for some time. Ever since the first contact with the French, the Indians had been seeking to bring the colony to the Mobile River. For selfish reasons, they needed the colonists for protection against the encroachments of rival tribes such as the Creeks and the Alabamas. And they loved the trinkets that the French lavishly bestowed on them.

But the Mobile Indians had something to offer the French. They could show them how to till the soil, how to make their way in the wilderness and more importantly they could aid the French in their plans to trade with the Indians of the interior. In the battle with England for control of North America, commerce with the Indians was to be the prized bone of contention. And the area where the competition would broil most heatedly was the valley of the Alabama-Tombigbee River that emptied into the Mobile. Here the English and the French trader would vie for the good favor of the American savage.

It was a battle that Iberville could foresee with poignant clarity. What more strategic move could be made, then, than to found a colony near the mouth of this coveted river basin? Already, he had secured the port at Dauphin Island. Now that Sauvole and Bienville had given their recommendations, it only remained for Iberville to give the command and the axes would begin to chop.

Laying ill with fever at Pensacola, Iberville made his decision. He dispatched two vessels to Fort Maurepas, a ketch with supplies for the new fort and a launch with eighty workers. Two weeks later, on January 12, 1702, the ketch returned from Maurepas along with a traversier, reporting that Bienville had arrived at Dauphin Island with forty men. A few months before, Sauvole had died at Maurepas and Bienville advanced to commandant. Now Iberville ordered his brother to commence operations and Bienville put his carpenters to work. They cleared the land in a matter of days and began construction of the houses and buildings.

Meanwhile, Iberville recovered from his fever and landed at Dauphin Island where he supervised the building of that port. For the next few weeks he was busy directing the transfer of supplies from Maurepas to the new site. Then Iberville arrived at the site, himself, where he spent the month of March, 1702, in directing the building of the fort. During that month, the fort called Fort Louis de la Louisiane was virtually completed and Iberville, on the last day of March, departed for France, relinquishing personal command of that vast enterprise in the new world that he had begun at Fort Maurepas. Now Fort Louis of the Mobile was the capital of the Louisiana Territory and was to remain such for the next eight years until the transfer down-river to the edge of Mobile Bay in 1710. The man Iberville left in charge was his twenty-two year old brother, Jean-Baptiste Le Moyne, Sieur de Bienville.

Chapter 3

Monsieur Bienville
takes Command

Young Bienville was a serious fellow, ambitious, headstrong and domineering. If his detractors could accuse him of being petty and quarrelsome, they could never doubt his loyalty to the King nor his ambition for the new colony. Gazing into the next century, the young Bienville could envision an American Paris with its marvelous cathedrals, splendid castles and gay night life. Looking back towards the forests, he could see his finely built chateaus embroidered with iron lace and delicate rose gardens. Surely, Mobile would be the cultural and commercial center of the new world, reflecting the grandeur and glory of France.

But still it was 1702. The more down-to-earth Canadians and "coureurs de bois" could but see a plain, wooden stockade built on the river bluff. They could see the simple town laid out with the main streets running parallel to the river and the side streets intersecting at regular intervals. Between the town proper and the fort, they could see the Place Royalle, where the garrison would hold military parades. And two blocks away could be seen the marche, a public square with a small well in the center. Further back from the river were the barracks for the soldiers, a hospital and a seminary and a warehouse for the supplies sent by the king. Behind the town in the piney woods, a cemetery lay waiting for the weak of body and spirit.

The cemetery didn't have long to wait. Disease reared its ugly head the first year and gave the new graveyard a couple of customers. The next year a few more Frenchmen bit the dust and by 1704 the new graveyard was doing a whopping business due to an unwelcome visitor called yellow fever. It was suspected to have stowed away on the good ship *Pelican* and, before it departed the colony, had carried off a goodly number of the colonists.

One of its victims was the most popular man in America, Henri de Tonty. This gallant soldier had fought innumerable battles in the old world before tackling those of the new. He left behind a hand in Europe but picked up an iron one and carried it to America where he joined La Salle in exploring the Southwest. Soon he was caught up in La Salle's vision of a French colony in the valley of the Mississippi. Above all others, Tonty was idolized by Frenchman and savage alike. The admiration of the Indians could be well understood since he was known far and wide as "the man with the built-in tomahawk." When La Salle was murdered, Tonty kept the dream alive. For a long, discouraging decade, before Iberville had made his mark, while Bienville was still a child, Tonty, alone, had carried visions in his head, constantly petitioning the King to found a colony in Louisiana. Of Tonty, alone, could it be said that he ran the gamut of empire from dream to fulfillment. Now, in

1704, secure in the knowledge of his accomplishment, he was gently laid away in the old cemetery on Twenty-Seven Mile Bluff, leaving behind a multitude of aggrieved Mobilians.

Soon after the epidemic, the Cure La Vente arrived in Mobile and began the keeping of the Church records; marriages, births, baptisms and deaths, records which are still in existence. Le Vente baptized several of the new-born Mobile Indians whose parents had been converted to Christianity. He must also have performed some marriage ceremonies among the colonists for on October 4, 1704, he baptized François le Camp, the first Créole listed in the baptismal records. Little François was always thought to have been the first Créole, but in 1731, in New Orleans, a curious trial was held to determine just who had been the first of the French to be born in Louisiana. At the trial, Jean-Baptiste Baudreau de la Graveline and several others who had lived at old Mobile testified unanimously that the first Créole was Claude Jousette de La Loire born in Mobile in early 1704. Claude, himself, then twenty-seven years old, was at the trial and likewise testified that he was the first Créole. Of course, Claude only knew what he had been told but who was the judge to tell a man when he had been born. And so the case was decided.

As for the mother of La Loire, she must have been one of those hearty souls who had the temerity to brave the wilderness before the first boatload of ladies landed. The lack of women was indeed an acute thorn in the side of Bienville. The lecherous behavior of the Frenchmen toward the Indian girls was causing some dangerous friction between the French and Indians, even though it gave the priests good material for their sermons. Bienville asked the authorities in France for some remedy and the answer was soon forthcoming.

The fall of 1704 welcomed a strange shipload of cargo. When the *Pelican* docked at Old Mobile, down the planks stepped daintily no less than twenty-three damsels from France. Some were pretty, some were not. But it hardly mattered. All were well dressed and toting a little trunk called a cassette, given to them by the King to aid them in the seducing of husbands. The Frenchmen needed no extra incentive, though. One can well picture the eye-bugging that must have followed when the girls were introduced to their prospective bridegrooms. The men were anxious, yet timid and rusty in technique of courtship. But no matter. They were married so quickly that it was a moot question as to who seduced whom!

The young wives appeared to be content, as time went on, except in one notable instance. They couldn't stomach this stuff the Mobilians called "corn bread." In what has since been called "The Petticoat Rebellion," the Cassette girls staged America's first sit-in. They refused to get off their rumps until their husbands planted some "French bread." The men of Mobile, of course, then took time out for farming. They had early discovered what future generations of Americans would later find out for themselves, that women in cahoots are a woeful opposition! But the couples survived that early conflict and became the progenitors of thousands of present-day Mobilians. To a woman, the Cassette girls remained with their husbands. Evidently they had decided that a double bed in the woods is worth any number of single beds in Paris.

By 1706 Mobile had received a few more colonists, had taken a census and seemed to be thriving. But that year Bienville received a severe jolt to his ambitions. His brother Iberville died of yellow fever in Havana. From whence would his support now come in the battles that would have to be fought in the French Court for finances and supplies? While Tonty and Iberville had been pleading his case to the government, Bienville's task had been a cut and dried problem of local administration. Now, at the age of twenty-six, the fortunes of Louisiana weighed heavy on his young shoulders.

There was more to come. Ever since Bienville had taken command, a pair of envious eyes in the person of one Nicholas de la Salle had been set on the commandant's position. La Salle had been appointed by the King to the position of intendant in charge of finances. It was a powerful office and one that diluted the executive power of Bienville. La Salle's reports to the King charging Bienville with inefficiency and malfeasance were so convincing that the King removed both Bienville and La Salle. The next year the new intendant, Martin D'Artaguette, arrived but the new governor had died at Havana. Now Bienville would be obliged to remain in office. He took great pains to stay on the good side of D'Artaguette, much to the chagrin of La Salle, and soon it was clear to all that Bienville had won the first battle of a long series of diplomatic intrigues. A few years later Bienville had a far more serious run-in with a much higher official than La Salle. But for now his position was secure even if his problems were mounting.

One of the commandant's troubles was the lack of something to fill the colonial belly. Supply ships were few and far between. In the meantime, Bienville was expected to live off the fat of the land. But the land was not so fat. Several colonists were sent to mooch off the Indians, when the times became extremely lean. One of the ships expected to bring a plethora of supplies was the ship called *St. Antoine.* Commanded by St. Maurice of St. Malo, she gracefully bore as a figure-head on her bow a wooden figure of St. Antoine. Perhaps tiring of all the saints involved, the sailors irreverently dislodged the figure, tied a stone around its neck and tossed it into the sea. But a few hours later, just as the ship was nearing the edge of Dauphin Island, a storm blew up and a disastrous shipwreck gave St. Antoine his revenge.

So much for Bienville's food supply. Now he must go back to the berries and the corn bread and send a few more colonists to the Indians. By this time, Bienville was finding his native American friends a bit exasperating. The great Tonty was able to unite the surrounding tribes in a notable congress in Mobile. But no figure of the stature of Tonty was around to look after them now. A Pascagoula Indian killed a Mobile and the Mobiles declared war on the Pascagoulas. Bienville soon straightened out that rivalry but then a Mobilian killed a Creek and the Creeks attacked the Apalachees. Worst of all the commander began to be troubled by that vicious band from the North, the savage Chickasaws who once had wreaked havoc on DeSoto and who, three decades hence, would destroy Bienville's career in Louisiana.

But now, in 1710, Bienville was fearfully watching the floodwaters of a rising Mobile river.

Chapter 4

Mobile Moves Downstream

It was something that the Mobile Indians neglected to tell Bienville; that is, that the Mobile River was, likely as not, to rise up and spill itself over the surrounding lowlands. Nevertheless, here was the Paris-to-be of the New World up to its neck in muddy water. Now Bienville was asking himself, "How long is this going to go on?"

Taking no chances, he canoed down river and his eyes lighted on a flat piece of land at the point where the river runs into the bay. It wasn't exactly what he wanted but no matter. It was the best he could find. The order went out: "Move the city!" The axemen swiftly leveled the trees and Bienville was soon engrossed in the building of new Mobile.

Another Fort Louis was erected in short order. Then the streets were laid out and the colonists built themselves some houses. Just to the south of the fort, Bienville built a house for himself and further down the

bay he completed something that had occupied his idle
waking moments for several years. Near what Mobilians of today call Garrow's Bend, the dashing commander built a chateau for his summer residence. It
was no stone castle, of course, and perhaps any French
nobleman would have snickered at the rustic attempt
at elegance. But it was comfortable and cool and it had
a garden on the grounds. From the balcony Bienville
could sit in the breeze and watch the ships sailing back
and forth from Dauphin Island. It would be a fine place
to relax while he supervised the building of Mobile into
a great port.

But Bienville was to have little time to relax. Food
was getting scarce, the men were demanding more
women and the English were beginning to cross the
Southern frontier in an effort to horn in on the Indian
trade. Bienville was soon reporting to Pontchartrain that
"we are not able to sustain ourselves any longer against
the flood of presents which the English offer them to
abandon our side. It is two years since we have given
the Indians anything, and during that time we have
kept them hoping from month to month."

Supplies were not forthcoming because France herself was in dire straits. By the second year of New
Mobile's existence, Louisiana was an obvious victim of
reckless exploitation and Europe's distresses. But to the
rescue came the empire merchant Antoine de Crozat. He
leased the whole colony from the King in return for all
the profits and now proceeded to bleed Louisiana dry.
He sent over a new Governor named Cadillac and Bienville was stripped of his power. Almost immediately the
two leaders were at each other's throats. One of Cadillac's
secretaries copied verbatim the dialogue of a heated argument and sent the transcripts to Pontchartrain:

Bienville: You told Monsieur Le Bart that I told you

that he was the one who wrote the letter to Monsieur Duclos that started the quarrel between you two.

Cadillac: Yes, you told me that.

Bienville: No, I did not tell you that.

Cadillac: Yes, indeed, you told me that. I'm not making it up.

Bienville: I didn't tell you that at all.

Cadillac: How are you speaking to me, Sir?

Bienville: I am speaking very politely. You are the one who is speaking badly.

Cadillac: What, by God, I am speaking badly? You are an impertinent fellow and I order you to shut up.

Bienville: It makes no difference to me. I'm not too impressed that you should order me to shut up.

Cadillac: You are now under arrest. You will go away immediately.

Bienville: I will do no such thing.

Cadillac: We shall see about that. (Speaking to his son) Go tell the Major to come here.

Bienville: Where do you wish me to go under arrest?

Cadillac: To your house, Monsieur.

Bienville: That's all right but it's still too early. (Now the Major arrives.) Here is the Major, Monsieur. What do you wish to do about it?

Cadillac: Take Monsieur Bienville to his house under arrest.

Bienville: So much the better. That should refresh me if we are there long, for we are now in the hot season.

Lofty words for men shaping the destiny of empires! But the noblest of men, in their unguarded moments, are sometimes given to the ways of popinjays.

Cadillac soon after had a further reason to be incensed at Bienville. His young daughter, charming and educated in France, fell in love with Bienville. Thinking of something feminine to grace his new chateau, Bienville seriously began to consider marriage. He mentioned this possibility to several of his colleagues, then wrote a letter to his brother seeking advice. The news leaked out and Cadillac sent for Bienville. Much as Cadillac despised the youthful arrogance of Bienville, he recognized the political value of such a union. When, at great expense to his pride, he offered his daughter's hand to Bienville, he was sorely chagrined. Bienville appeared to be surprised. Indifferently, the young Le Moyne replied that he was not so much interested in marrying anyone at all at this time.

What changed Bienville's mind no one can imagine but it is easy to visualize the wrath of the Governor. How could anyone, especially a barbaric Canadian, turn down a Cadillac? Bienville must have had his reasons but the furious Cadillac now determined to send Bienville to his death. With only a handful of men, he ordered Bienville to the Natchez country. The war-like Natchez had recently murdered four Frenchmen and it was to punish those vicious savages that Cadillac sent Bienville with but thirty-four men. However, the wiley Bienville captured several of the Natchez leaders, then made peace with the rest of the Indians and returned to Mobile a hero. Cadillac was beside himself with anger but his troubles had just begun. It seems that Crozat had finally given up the idea of Louisiana as a profit-making enterprise and had turned the colony back over to the King. Cadillac was partly blamed for the fiasco, recalled to France and chucked into prison to cool off for a while. Bienville was once more in the driver's seat.

If Bienville expected any new problems, he didn't have long to wait. As soon as Cadillac had departed, the savage hurricane of 1717, one of the worst in colonial history, struck Mobile Bay. It almost cut Dauphin Island in half and sealed up the port with sand. Mobile was left with no safe anchorage for ships and it soon became apparent to Bienville that Mobile's future was in jeopardy.

Then another cloud appeared on the horizon. Spain and France were at war! A ship from Europe had just brought the news. Quickly, Bienville moved against Pensacola, suspecting that they had not yet learned of the war. He was right. The Frenchmen easily captured Pensacola and Bienville returned to Mobile, leaving his brother Chateaugué to supervise the prisoners. But it wasn't long before the Viceroy of Mexico sent a strong fleet to recapture Pensacola and Chateaugué was sent to Havana and tossed in the dungeons.

In the midst of all Bienville's problems, the great King Louis died and was succeeded by his infant great-grandson. The Duke of Orleans, making most of the young King's decisions, turned the colony over to a Scotch gambler named John Law. Law's grand scheme was to sell stock to private investors in a venture that he called The West India Company. These investors would share the profits from all the gold and furs that would surely flow into France.

Bienville soon was meeting thousands of colonists who had come over to strike it rich. He must have received the new immigrants with mixed emotions. Certainly he needed the manpower but he grimaced at the thought of the disappointment that was inevitable when they discovered the lack of precious metals in Louisiana.

Bienville had his own problems to contend with at this particular point in his career. Foremost among these was what to do with Mobile. Before his departure, Cadillac had taken one last look at Mobile and declared, "the entire colony is nothing but sand, fit only for hour glasses." Now the hurricane had ruined the port at Dauphin Island. In 1718, Bienville had gone back to the Mississippi and founded the city of New Orleans but he was not yet ready to abandon Mobile. It was too valuable as a trading post to be cast aside so lightly. And the town had by this time grown to nearly a thousand inhabitants. Finally, as all the large ships were forced to anchor at Ship Island, his decision became clear. He would keep Mobile as a trading post but the capital must be moved back to Biloxi. By 1721, Mobile was all but forgotten as Bienville carried his seat of government to Biloxi and then on to New Orleans.

While Bienville was busy developing New Orleans, Mobile was left behind to grow on its own. It lost a few residents almost immediately. Jean-Baptiste Baudreau de la Graveline and Joseph Simon de la Pointe, two wealthy citizens who had lived at Mobile from the very beginning, moved to the west and founded the town of Pascagoula. A few Mobilians moved further up the river and Monsieur Minette moved across the swamps and found a serene little bay on which to settle.

Still a few immigrants were moving into Mobile. In the year 1721, a shipload of German colonists landed at Mobile looking for a quiet place to settle, far from strife-torn Europe. One young lady among the colonists stood out rather distinctively from all the rest. She was of a comely appearance, exquisitely garbed, and apparently well-off financially. Mobilians were whispering that this damsel was none other than the daughter of the

Duke of Brunswick Wolfenbuttel and the wife of Alexis Petrowitz, eldest son of Peter the Great, czar of Russia. She was soon referred to as "The Princess of Mobile."

The princess related a sad story of how she had been beaten by her vicious husband and so cruelly treated that she was forced to flee the country. She secretly went to Germany and joined the colonists embarking for Mobile. Now, here she was in the French outpost in search of a new life away from the trials and tribulations of royalty.

The young woman's story was easily believed by the Mobilians. Her dress, her money and her courtly manner was indication enough that she was indeed of a wealthy and aristocratic family. Her amazing knowledge of intrigues and skeletons of the court closet gave her story a further note of credibility. But it was a dashing young French officer, the Chevalier d'Aubant who set in motion one of the most extraordinary hoaxes in history. D'Aubant declared that he had with his own eyes seen the wife of Peter the Great's son when he was stationed in St. Petersburg and that the Princess was indeed that very lady.

During the following months, d'Aubant watched the princess for hours on end as she sat brooding under the oaks of Mobile. His sympathy soon grew into something more and before long he began a courtship that resulted in the marriage of d'Aubant and the princess. For a number of years they lived in Mobile and the princess bore the chevalier a daughter. Years later, the family moved to Paris where d'Aubant died.

The princess lived to be an old woman before the hoax was finally exposed by none other than the great Voltaire. One day she was walking in the Tuileries gardens in Paris when she encountered the Marshall of

Saxe who recognized her and reported it to his friend Voltaire who publicly exposed her to the European press. In reality, she was a female attendant of the deceased wife of the Czar's son. When the real princess disappeared, the pretender saw her opportunity and with the enormous amount of money, jewels and clothes she stole from her mistress, was able to carry off the masquerade. d'Aubant died in blissful ignorance of his wife's true origin, never doubting for a moment that he was married to a real princess. She died in poverty but not without the satisfaction that the world recognized her ingenious way of capturing a husband. The fake princess was the first in line of a long list of Mobile women who would capture the hearts of men everywhere with their beauty, charm and resourcefulness.

While all this was going on, Monsieur Bienville had been back and forth between Paris and Mobile. John Law's bubble had burst wide open and Bienville was recalled to France to answer for his part in the failure. By 1733, Bienville was back in Mobile planning the last great military campaign of his career. His hated enemies, the British, were overflowing across the mountains and striking up an alliance with the Chickasaw Indians who were trying to turn the other Southern Indians, the Creeks, the Choctaws and the Alabamas, against the French. Now, at this late hour in his career, there was one last chance to stifle the growth of England. He must attack the Chickasaws on their home base and annihilate them.

Early one morning in the year 1736, Bienville left Mobile with raw and ragged troops, ascended the Tombigbee River and engaged the Chickasaw Indians in ferocious combat. It was soon apparent that the Frenchmen were no match for the Chickasaws. Bienville was soundly defeated and, in fact, lucky to escape with his life. Disgustedly, he drifted back to Mobile. It was the beginning of the end for the fifty-six-year-old commander. In 1743, he resigned from office and returned to Paris where he spent the rest of his life advocating support for the colony. He died in 1767, unsung and forgotten. Of the founder of Mobile it could well be said that of all the careers of the world's great leaders, none, for singleness of purpose, could match that of Jean-Baptiste Le Moyne, Sieur de Bienville. He never married a woman. He married a colony and an empire.

Chapter 5

Créoles and the Union Jack

Mobile slumbered on for the next twenty years following Bienville's departure. Fort Condé, built by Bienville and Cadillac in 1717, became more useful than ever. Once, Mobilians took pride in their lack of fear of the Indians. Now a mischievous savage called Red Shoe was laying waste to settlers on the outskirts of Mobile. When Red Shoe was killed in 1748, Mobilians breathed a sigh of relief but there were soon other renegade Indians to take his place. The city folks palisaded themselves in and dreamed of brighter days when Mobile would grow into a flowering Paris.

Prospects looked pretty dim in the middle of the eighteenth century. Mobile was not the thriving settlement she once was in the days of Bienville. There were only a couple hundred residents and half of these were slaves. The French and Swiss soldiers in the garrison outnumbered the residents in the city. Even the elements seemed to be thwarting its growth. The hurricane of

1740 lit into Dauphin Island and tore it completely in half, killing livestock and damaging buildings in Mobile. But it was neither wind nor disease nor famine that was governing the fate of the city by the bay. Mobile's destiny was being decided from afar by the increasing power of England, and inwardly by the demoralizing conduct of the colony's officials.

In the last years of the French and Indian War, as Bienville sat brooding his life away in Paris, an incident occurred in the colony exemplifying the corruption of France's colonial leaders. One of the central figures in this dramatic episode was the son of an illustrious Canadian named Jean-Baptiste Baudreau de la Graveline. Graveline had settled at Maurepas with Iberville, then moved over to Twenty-Seven Mile Bluff and built a home near Bienville. In 1711 he moved down to new Mobile and eight years later settled on the Pascagoula River where he owned all the land between that river and Biloxi Bay. Baudreau de la Graveline was one of the wealthiest, most loyal colonists in the new world. When he died, he bequeathed his good name to his son who was settled on Cat Island in 1757. This Baudreau, a giant, native Louisianian, lived with his wife, three sons and a daughter on the island from which he would often venture onto the mainland in search of excitement. Once he tracked down three Creek Indians who were kidnapping a planter near Mobile. Baudreau killed the three Creeks and brought his friend safely back to Mobile. Another time, he had rescued a compatriot on the Mobile River from a band of maurauding Chickasaws. All in all, he was a well-respected frontiersman, even beloved by the Indians when he wasn't killing them.

Over on nearby Ship Island lived the Commander Duroux with whom Baudreau had already undergone

one dispute. Baudreau, it seems, had spied the wreckage of a Spanish ship some months before and had removed some of the spoils; a keg of wine, an iron pot, and a few other articles. Duroux was enraged that Baudreau had failed to consult him and threw the frontiersman into chains. Under Duroux's command was a company of Swiss soldiers whom he worked to the bone and generally subjected to the rigors of Hades. When some of the soldiers escaped to New Orleans, they lodged a complaint to Governor de Kerlerec, who unsympathetically returned them to the chains of Duroux.

The commandant's discipline reached such unbearable proportions that when he went on a hunting trip to Deer Island, the soldiers planned a mutiny. Plainly, the brutality of Duroux had gone far enough. When late in the afternoon the commandant returned, the Swiss soldiers were ready. As soon as Duroux stepped off the ship, the garrison saluted, presented arms and shot him dead. Then the mutineers stripped his body clean and tossed him into the Gulf.

Frantically, the soldiers approached Baudreau. Would he guide them overland to the safety of the English colonies? Baudreau knew well the fate of an accomplice to a murder of a French commandant. He offered them advice but the panic-stricken assassins took the reluctant guide along forcibly. Seizing the ships, the fugitives made their way to Dauphin Island where they ditched the boats and hiked to Mobile. Among friends, Baudreau procured some canoes and the party paddled its way up the Alabama River, finally reaching Coweta on the Chattahoochee.

Baudreau and the Swiss soldiers parted at that point but not before the Swiss had given Baudreau a written statement that he was in no way responsible for the murder of Duroux and that he had been forcibly retained as a guide.

Baudreau, feeling somewhat secure, returned to Mobile. The Swiss soldiers split into two parties, one group safely reaching Carolina. But the other party was finally tracked down by an expedition of Indians sent out by the commander of Fort Toulouse. The captured assassins were then shipped down to Mobile and thrown in a dungeon to await trial.

One day Baudreau's sons arrived in Mobile with a sealed envelope sent to Commander De Ville of Mobile by Governor de Kerlerec. Unknown to Baudreau's sons, the envelope contained orders for the arrest of Baudreau. The unfortunate guide was then led to a cell in Fort Conde where, to his utter amazement, he found the Swiss soldiers staring back at him in terror.

The trial was short and to the point. Baudreau was found guilty of cooperating in the murder of Duroux. He was taken outside in front of the gates of Fort Condé, where his father once lived so honorably. In full view of hundreds of his Mobile friends and relatives, Baudreau was strapped to a giant wheel which slowly began to turn him around and drag him through the spikes, breaking his body. Then the mutilated corpse was thrown into the Mobile River. The Swiss murderers were nailed into separate coffins. One was buried alive and the other was sawed in half.

It was a pathetic end for one whose father had contributed so much to the colony. But in death Baudreau had a sort of revenge. His surviving daughter married Joseph Bosarge and together they founded the town of Bayou La Batre. And for just such wrongdoings, Governor de Kerlerec was recalled to France and thrown in the Bastille.

The tide had turned too far, however, for France to save her mismanaged colony. The English captured Quebec, then blockaded Mobile Bay. In a secret treaty in 1762, France ceded Louisiana to Spain but the English, with a firm grip on Mobile, refused to give up that port. The next year, a doddering octogenerian named Bienville made a valiant effort to save Mobile from the English, but his cries fell on deaf ears as the French Government signed the Treaty of Paris by which Mobile was organized as a part of British West Florida. The commandant of Mobile, Pierre De Ville, delivered his city to an English major named Robert Farmer. A new era was dawning for the port city.

Major Farmer was a mere lad of twenty-eight when he waved the Union Jack over Mobile. He took one look at Fort Condé and decided it needed overhauling. The glass windows were gone, the grounds grown up in weeds and the gun platforms had fallen down. After the major had repaired the Fort, he insulted the French inhabitants by changing its name to Fort Charlotte in honor of the young queen of George III. To add injury to insult he then held the first Protestant Church service inside the walls and nailed a proclamation to the main gate giving the French residents of Mobile three months in which to take the oath of allegiance to the English king.

Needless to say, Major Farmer was not an object of affection among the Créoles. Some of them went to New Orleans to escape him but most of them retired to homes on the bay and the river. They extracted a promise from Farmer that no private property would be confiscated, which was fine with the Major until he discovered that his own house was on a private tract. Furious but true to his word, Major Farmer was forced to rent a house until he could buy some land across the bay from the savages. He built a house on an Indian mound and lived out his life on that plantation near modern-day Stockton.

Major Farmer took a short leave of absence from his Mobile post and ascended the Mississippi River. He had a bit more success on that river and it wasn't long before he had taken possession of the whole Northwest. When he came back to Mobile, he found that he had Indian trouble. It seems that the Indians didn't care for the British. "The Englishmen were stingy and discriminating," the Indians claimed. Besides, they didn't have a sense of humor like the Frenchmen.

The Mobile Indians had turned up their noses at the new faces and went to Louisiana the same year that the English had taken possession. When several other tribes followed suit, Farmer decided that his trading business was in serious trouble. Reluctantly, he called upon a Frenchman. Chevalier Montaut de Monberaut was Commander at Fort Toulouse when the French surrendered Louisiana but unlike other French officials, he remained in British territory. Governor Johnstone at Pensacola requested that Farmer find an Indian agent and Monberaut was called upon to undertake the difficult task of reconciling the Indians and the British.

Being a Catholic, it was impossible for Monberaut to be employed, according to British law. Farmer suggested that Monberaut change his religion but the Frenchman only attempted to convert Farmer. It was finally decided that Monberaut should be only an advisor with unusual powers. After taking the King's oath, Monberaut warned his employers of the expense of seducing Indians, after which the Frenchman fixed up a large house in Mobile and made it a veritable casino. He entertained the Indians as if they had been the crowned heads of Europe. There was feasting, wine and revelry every day at Monberaut's. Even John Stuart, the Governor's Indian agent, occasionally dropped in to witness the fanfare. Stuart had a bad case of the gout but, when he got his belly full of wine, he often-times danced all night. Monberaut once commented that Stuart behaved as if he had been bitten by a tarantula.

After the Indians had thus been feted and wined, Monberaut and Major Farmer called for a great Indian Congress. The Creeks and the Choctaws descended on Mobile in great numbers. Chieftains, squaws and papooses bulged the city's population to twice its size. Since the Creeks and the Choctaws were not on such friendly terms not many Mobilians were surprised when a band of Choctaw braves went on the warpath and chased three hundred Creeks down the main streets of Mobile and all the way into the river. At the end of Government Street, the Choctaws suddenly came to a screeching halt. The townsfolk soon perceived the reason. The Choctaws were great land-lubbers but they couldn't swim.

Despite the occasional outbreak of violence, the Congress was a success. The English gave up guns and the Indians gave up land. When the conference was over, Governor Johnstone was overjoyed until he discovered that Monberaut and Farmer had bled his finances dry in the process. The Governor gave Monberaut three days to get out of Mobile and Major Farmer was courtmartialed. Monberaut went to New Orleans where he became known as "The Count," but the Major was made to suffer the indecencies of a trial. He was charged with embezzling ten thousand pounds, selling Fort Tombecbé to a charlatan, and stealing the king's flour. For some reason, Major Farmer was acquitted. But then he quit Mobile and went to live across the Bay for the rest of his life.

After Farmer and Monberaut left Mobile, the English

had little trouble from the Indians. But they didn't have much cooperation, either. Especially in matters of the Protestant denomination. When the Anglican Reverend Hart came from Charleston to win the Indians over to the faith of the King, he found a vexing barrier between himself and his prey.

"Where does this God Almighty live?" asked an old Indian chief to whom the Reverend was pleading his case. "And is he a friend of Brother George?"

The Clergyman was in the midst of a windy explanation when the old Indian broke in on his discourse. "Beloved friend," said the chief, "I will always admire this friend of yours, God Almighty, of whom you speak so well. Let us drink to his health."

The Reverend shook his head and wondered how the Catholic Clergyman had ever gotten through to these amazing people.

The English managed to hold on to Mobile for awhile but between the Indians and the uncooperative Créoles, their enthusiasm was diminishing. William Bartram, the British naturalist, came canoeing into Mobile in 1777 and a few years before, Bernard Romans made a sashay through Mobile. Both of these distinguished visitors found the colony to be in fairly good shape but their ears were not so keen. Had they been attuned to the times they could have heard the rumblings of revolt in Virginia and the murmurings of intrigue in New Orleans.

Chapter 6

The Spaniards Try Pot Luck

The American colonies were revolting! The shot heard 'round the world made a big noise in the East but it bounced off the walls of Fort Charlotte with a flat thud. Mobilians' sympathies went out to the colonists but surrounded by English bayonets, there was little else they could offer. They watched helplessly as agents from Virginia, trying to sneak into the city to circulate the Declaration of Independence, were captured and thrown into the dungeons.

Young Bernardo de Galvez, the Spanish Governor of Louisiana, was not so timid. Sensing his opportunity, he made a dash up the Mississippi and seized Baton Rouge from the English. The next year, he landed his ships on the shores of Mobile Bay and was soon knocking at the doors of Fort Charlotte. At the arrival of Galvez, the entire city of Mobile, Créoles and Britons alike, rushed inside the fort and waited for Galvez to make his move.

It wasn't long in coming. Ever the unpredictable one, Bernardo sent an envoy on a drinking expedition. Waving a flag of truce, Colonel Bolyny, was received into the fort with cordiality. He immediately proposed a toast to George III, and Captain Durnford, the English Commandant, issued a toast to the Spanish King. They then proposed a toast to one another which they quickly acted upon, then a toast to all Spaniards and each Créole and every Englishman. When all had thus been properly toasted and the two leaders had attained a spritely mood, the Spanish Envoy politely suggested to Durnford that he surrender. The English Commandant politely refused and after another toast, the Spanish Envoy returned to Galvez and the guns began to roar. Surely, the gallant touch still had its place, even in the midst of the clashing of empires.

On the first day of siege Captain Durnford called his men together, read Galvez's demand to them, and announced that if any soldier wished to surrender, he could freely walk out the gates and hand over his sword. None did, of course, and the captain read aloud his message of refusal to surrender. The garrison responded with rousing shouts of defiance and bravely the English braced themselves to withstand the siege. After thirteen days of bombardment, Captain Durnford looked at the huge holes in Fort Charlotte's walls and decided it was an unlucky day. His stickmen struck up the drums, his ropeman pulled up a pale flag and the small garrison of red coats marched out the front door and stacked their arms. Galvez had taken Mobile. For the next thirty years the port city would be Spanish.

Across Mobile Bay, a Pensacola expedition had been on the way to rescue Captain Durnford. But hearing of the Captain's surrender, the rescue party fled to Pensacola, and Galvez, in order to prevent the return of the

English built a fort that still stands and has since ever been known as the Old Spanish Fort.

Under the rule of Spain, Mobile took on a new look. All the new buildings constructed were clearly recognizable as Spanish in design. Blocks of low, wide-spreading houses began to appear over the city, replacing many of the old Créole and English edifices that, in time, crumbled to earth.

And the Spaniards felt a curious urge to change the names of streets, which confused the citizens as well as the mailman. St. Charles became San Emanuel and Conti became San Pedro. St. Michael became San Iago and Dauphin Street was changed to San Juan. The Spanish apparently intended to give the whole town to the Saints! It wasn't until thirty years later when the Americans came that it was turned over to the Presidents.

The Catholic Church was re-established as the official church of Mobile. In fact, it was the only one tolerated. Protestants were told to get out of town or keep it to themselves. Spanish became the official language but most Mobilians went right on speaking "La Langue Français."

The Negroes fared a little better under the Spaniards. They were still bought and sold but were often allowed to work out their freedom and some free Negroes even owned their own slaves. One military company was composed entirely of mulattoes and free blacks. Its commander, P. J. Lusser, was a soldier of such merit that his widow, a free Negro, was eventually presented with a fine home near Fort Charlotte.

The end of the Revolutionary War brought a confusion of boundary lines between the claims of England, Spain and the United States. The disputed territory was inhabited and controlled by the Creek Indians and none of the three nations had enough soldiers to seriously occupy the lands. The result was a war of diplomacy between the disputants and the man whose favor was being courted was the chief of the Creek Nation—a cunning half-breed named Alexander McGillivray.

This wily Indian, the son of a Scotch fur trader and a Creek princess, found himself in such an enviable position that he was able to live in luxury the year around. He made Mobile his summer headquarters and built himself a stylish summer home on Dog River. During the Revolution, McGillivray served as a British agent among the Indians. He sent out war parties against the American frontiersmen and when the war was over, became a silent partner in the Mobile trading house of Panton, Lesley and Company.

McGillivray had several avowed purposes in life. As far as his fellow Creeks knew, his life's ambition was to unite the southern Indians. Then, with the aid of Great Britain or Spain, he would force the Americans to restore the Indian boundaries as they once existed.

His private purpose was to keep the three major nations at each other's throats and to auction off his services to the highest bidder. He didn't have long to wait. George Washington made him a brigadier general at twelve hundred dollars a year. The British appointed him commandant of a fort in Alabama and the Spanish made him general of the Creek nation with a salary of thirty-five hundred dollars a year. For a decade, McGillivray dangled the three nations on a string and became an international figure. He started a war with the American frontiersmen, then forced Spain to send him munitions to save him from defeat. After Spain came to his rescue, McGillivray expressed a wish that all the Creek towns be organized as a state and be admitted into the Union. President Washington called him to New York and there

McGillivray signed a treaty with the United States. In return for a pension of $1,200 a year, he agreed to disregard the Creek-Spanish treaty of 1784.

When McGillivray returned to Mobile, he found his Spanish friends outraged but, nevertheless, willing to up the ante. When Spain offered McGillivray a thousand dollar increase in pension, the chieftain repudiated his treaty with Washington and worked the rest of his life trying to unite the Creeks against the United States, with financial assistance from Spain, of course. By added inducements from England, he was able to maintain three plantations, stock it with sixty slaves, and engage in a profitable cattle business. All his life, he lived well and was seldom out of debt. He admitted to two wives and was still drinking heavily when he died of a double dose of the gout and pneumonia while hatching a plot in Pensacola against the United States.

A few years after McGillivray died, the pot began to simmer in old Mobile. Spain's power was beginning to wane and she hastily concluded a treaty with the Americans which recognized the old line of 31° as the northern boundary of her lands in Florida. A Yankee engineer named Andrew Ellicott was sent to survey the boundary line. Using smoke to signal his assistants, he made his way through the dense forests north of Mobile and left a stone that is still the basis of surveying in South Alabama.

But now France was back in the picture, casting greedy glances at her lost territories in the new world. After exhausting Spain in the European Wars, Napoleon now demanded the return of *La Lousiane* and Spain was forced to hand it over. Would Mobile once again be French?

Not quite. The United States claimed Mobile was not

a part of the Louisiana territory granted to Spain by the Treaty of Paris in 1763. Therefore, what had not been given could not be returned. Spain readily agreed and with the backing of the United States held on to Mobile. Napoleon was in the midst of a vigorous protest when a revolution in Santo Domingo forced him to sell all of Louisiana to Thomas Jefferson. Now the tables were turned. The United States desperately wanted to add Mobile to her collection, but to now claim that Mobile was a part of the Louisiana acquisition would be just a little too much, even for the most spurious of logicians. Nevertheless, American expansionists had their lunch-hooks set and even optimistic Spaniards must have sensed the inevitable.

As the dawn of Spanish Mobile began to settle over the bay, three shadowy figures were inching their way toward the port city. From New Orleans, General James Wilkinson was setting the sails of his warships. From Natchez on the Mississippi, Aaron Burr was launching a grander scheme of conquest. And from the North, an unknown English judge was approaching the city.

Chapter 7

Harry Toulmin and Aaron Burr

Harry Toulmin didn't start life out as a judge. His father was the renowned English Unitarian, Josuah Toulmin. Young Harry early took up the cloak and was quickly ostracized from English society for his dissenting religious views. Looking for greener pastorates, Toulmin sailed from England with the equally heretical Joseph Priestly. Reaching America, Toulmin obtained a strong recommendation from Thomas Jefferson which led to an appointment as president of a seminary in Kentucky. After enduring for a time low wages and low esteem he took the former as an excuse to resign. From a chance political acquaintance, he found himself appointed Secretary of State of Kentucky. In that office Toulmin authored Kentucky's Code of Laws and promulgated the now famous Virginia-Kentucky Resolutions. Thus, the preacher-turned-politician became the staunch advocate of a new-fangled theory called "States Rights." A rebel in England, he was none the less in his adopted land.

But Harry Toulmin was not long for Kentucky. In 1798, the Mississippi Territory had been organized. Now, in 1804, Thomas Jefferson appointed Toulmin to the judgeship of the District. Locating himself at Ft. Stoddert on the Mobile River, just above the city of Mobile, Judge Toulmin set about his task with characteristic vigor. His main goal was to keep the Spanish in Mobile and to discourage Americans from trying to capture the city. Judge Toulmin wasn't always successful. Once a Spaniard named Kilcrease sneaked past Ellicott's stone and murdered a Créole. Then the villain slipped back across the line. Judge Toulmin, sensing the danger of such practices, appealed to the Spanish Governor of Mobile to release the murderer, promising a fair trial. When the Governor refused, Toulmin offered to supply him with evidence if he would see to it that the Spaniard was tried in Mobile. Toulmin's plea to the Governor was indicative of both his desire for peace and his reputation as a wind bag.

"I embrace this opportunity," he said, "Of doing myself the honor to assure you that I feel exceedingly solicitous that no facility should ever be afforded, by a difference of national jurisdictions between settlements so contiguous, to the vicious and abandoned on either side of the line to commit depredations with impunity . . . to cooperate in the suppression of villaintry and licentiousness."

Judge Toulmin kept General Wilkinson at bay but the designs of American expansionists were becoming more and more apparent. In 1807, the judge got wind of a supposed plot to capture Mobile. Aaron Burr, hero of the Revolution, ex-Vice-President of the United States and slayer of Alexander Hamilton, was on his way to Mobile from Natchez.

On a cold February night, two young men sat in

their cabin north of Mobile, playing a game of back-gammon. At ten o'clock they heard the tramp of hoof beats and presently a knock at the door. When they opened the door they could see two weary travelers, one of whom asked the way to the nearest tavern. Nicholas Perkins, a young lawyer, informed them of a place seven miles in the direction of Mobile. Looking them over carefully, his eyes lighted on a pair of strikingly beautiful boots protruding from under raggedy trousers. Then the fire suddenly blazed up and threw a bright light on the face of the man with the exquisite head. Observing closely, Perkins could see a noble face with sparkling eyes. Closing the door, he said to his backgammon partner, "That is Aaron Burr. I have read a description of him and I cannot be mistaken."

Unimpressed, his partner went back to his game. But Perkins jumped on his horse and rode to the Sheriff's house. Then Perkins and the Sheriff galloped to the inn and accosted the travelers. The Sheriff was unconvinced but Perkins' convictions were strengthened the more he thought about it. Thereupon, he rode to the Mobile River, borrowed a canoe and paddled down river to Fort Stoddert where he convinced Captain Edward P. Gaines to lead a detachment to cut off the man thought to be Aaron Burr.

Just after daybreak, the soldiers met the two mysterious travelers as they were coming over a hill. Captain Gaines stepped forward immediately.

"I presume, Sir," he said, "I have the honor of addressing Colonel Burr?"

"I am a traveler in the country," replied the stranger, "and do not recognize your right to ask such a question."

Captain Gaines took his evasive answer as an admission of his identity.

"I arrest you," he said, "at the instance of the Federal Government."

"By what authority do you arrest a traveler upon the highway?" asked the stranger.

"I am an officer of the Army," said Gaines. "I hold in my hands the proclamations of the President and the Governor, directing your arrest."

The stranger looked at the young captain coldly, then tried another line of attack.

"You are a young man," he said, "and may not be aware of the responsibilities which result from arresting travelers on private business."

"I am aware of the responsibilities," countered Captain Gaines, "but I know my duty."

Despite all of the stranger's eloquence in disclaiming his name, Captain Gaines only became the more convinced the longer the traveler talked. For what backwoodsman could speak so convincingly as this man?

Captain Gaines led Aaron Burr and his companion to Fort Stoddert where the celebrated prisoner played chess with Judge Toulmin's daughter and comforted the ailing George S. Gaines. Aaron was a popular prisoner, much more popular with Southerners than he had ever been back East. But soldiers have their duties and Burr was rowed up the Alabama River to be delivered to Federal authorities. On the way, the settlers came out to wave as he passed and one lady named a son after him. Back in the East, Burr was tried for treason, acquitted and ostracized. Nobody had proved what he was up to but he was roundly denounced, anyway—mainly for thinking about what the Government, itself, finally did.

If Judge Toulmin thought his troubles were gone

when Aaron Burr left the territory, he was sadly disillu-
sioned. In 1810, insurrection broke out and the West
Florida Republic came into being. Rueben Kemper captured Baton Rouge and descended on Mobile with a
wild, drunken war party. Judge Toulmin had him arrested, however, and Kemper's party was pooped. Rueben
described the judge as "a base Devil, filled with de-
ception and bloody rascality." Rueben Kemper's opinion of the judge was pretty well shared by most of the
Americans at this time. They were itching to get their
hands on Mobile and it was Harry Toulmin who seemed
to be thwarting their best efforts.

But now it was 1813. International politics was in a
tizzy. Napoleon was approaching Waterloo. Spain was
allying herself with England and the United States was
getting hacked off at the whole bloody bunch. When
Spain threw her ports on the Gulf open to the British,
President Madison ordered General Wilkinson to seize
Mobile. The General wasted little time and by April, 1813,
the American flag waved for the first time over the old
Latin city of Mobile and the Spaniards retreated to Pensacola.

Spain and England had their revenge, though, and
it wasn't long in coming. Enlisting the services of Red
Eagle, a halfbreed Indian whose English name was William Weatherford, the Spanish and English stirred the
wrath of the Indians against the white settlers. More
dangerous than McGillivray, more daring than Tucum-
seh, Red Eagle pounced upon a settlement across the bay
and up the river in Baldwin County called Fort Mims.
At high noon on August 30, 1813, in the full light of
day, one thousand Indians fell upon the unsuspecting
fort filled with men, women and children. When Red
Eagle sounded his retreat several hours later, the greatest massacre of white settlers in American history was

done. Over five hundred pioneers lay shot, scalped and burned in the ashes of Fort Mims.

The news of a massacre spread quickly through all the settlements in Alabama. The brave and fearful alike called for a hero to lead them in their lust for revenge. There were two who answered the call. Big Sam Dale was one. Singlehandedly, he killed twelve Indians in an epic canoe fight on the Alabama River and dogged the footsteps of the Creek warriors.

But the man of the hour was a Tennessee lawyer named Andrew Jackson. Old Hickory was idolized as much as any man ever was when he came into Alabama after the Fort Mims massacre to save the people from the savages. In a few months' time, Jackson tracked down Red Eagle and defeated him once and for all at the Battle of Horseshoe Bend. The Creek nation was crushed and Red Eagle surrendered. Floating down the Alabama River, Jackson came to Mobile and was wildly hailed as a conquering hero. Jackson had little time to waste resting on his laurels, however. The War of 1812 was in high gear by this time and Old Hickory set up military headquarters where the Battle House now stands. Looking to the southeast, he smelt a rat. The English in Pensacola, were planning a dastardly deed. Exactly what it was, Jackson did not know, but in a month's time, he rounded up his men and marched them to Pensacola. Easily capturing the Fort at Pensacola, Jackson returned to Mobile and awaited a turn of events.

It didn't take much of a strategist to figure out what the English were up to. General Packenham was moving his men and his ships to Dauphin Island. After a short encampment, Packenham struck his tents and set into motion the invasion of New Orleans. But Jackson had anticipated the British moves. Leaving Mobile, he marched across southern Mississippi and lodged himself firmly behind the cotton bales at Chalmette. Packenham was killed soon after the battle began and by nightfall Jackson and the Americans had won a decisive victory.

But the British lost no time in retreating to the Gulf. Back they went to Dauphin Island from whence they launched an attack on Fort Morgan, then called Fort Bowyer. Capturing the fort, the British were making further plans when news came that the war of 1812 was over. The British abandoned Mobile Bay, leaving behind in the sands scores of dead Britons who had finally succumbed from wounds sustained at New Orleans.

Chapter 8

Hail Lafayette!

During the last year of the war of 1812, Mobile was incorporated as a city. A couple of years later, Alabama became a territory and in 1819, the State of Alabama was created. Mobile was all set to undergo a profound change. The Americans were about to move in, full force.

In 1821, the old fort built by Bienville was destroyed. It was merely getting in the way since there was no longer any threat from Pensacola. However, across the bay, Mobile faced a new threat. Not from Spaniards or Englishmen or Indians but from an individual named Blakely.

Josiah Blakely had come to Mobile from Connecticut during the Spanish period. He took a close look at the bay area and decided that prospects were better in Baldwin County. On the other side of the bay, the river ran deeper and there was no competition for the land. He acquired a plantation and set about the task of building

a town that would put Mobile in the shade, a town he
humbly named after himself. He laid out the streets and
the avenues and after laying further plans, he lay down
and died. But Josiah's town went on without him. A bank
was opened and a newspaper was established. In short
order, a boom town was raising eyebrows in Mobile. By
1824 Blakely was a serious commercial competitor to her
sister city across the bay and hundreds of Mobilians
contemplated moving to the thriving new center. The
prosperity was short-lived. Back of the city and into the
ravine, the city's waste flowed. And from out of that
drainage point rose the pestilence of yellow fever. The
spring that supplied the city water became polluted and
the graveyard was soon receiving customers. By 1828,
Blakely was a ghost town lined with weeds and tomb-
stones. The stones are still there today and Washington
Avenue may be found by the now mature rows of oak
trees planted by Josiah Blakely just before he died.

In the spring of 1825, the city of Mobile was elec-
trified to learn that the great Lafayette was coming. A
half-century after Bunker Hill, the old warriors of the
Revolution were gone. Of those towering figures, only
Lafayette still lived. Seventy years old, insolvent, in disfavor in his native France, Lafayette was returning to
America in a blaze of glory at the invitation of Congress.
As he passed through the interior of North America, he
drove villages into hysterics by his mere presence.
Ladies waved their flags and old soldiers wept. By the
time he reached the capital of Alabama at Cahaba, the
Governor and all the young state's dignitaries were there
to greet him. Sailing down the Alabama River, Lafayette
doffed his hat to settlers of the river plantations. On the
fifth of April, 1825, his ship docked at the foot of Government Street. Met by Mayor Garrow and the entire
city, Lafayette stepped off the boat and into a carriage

which rolled him up and down the streets of Old Mobile. A triumphal arch was thrown across Dauphin Street and over Royal Street. After an hour of fanfare, the carriage came to a halt in front of a little hotel on the corner of Conti and Royal Streets. After the Mayor made a grand speech, Lafayette was rolled to Conception Street to the old Spanish Governor's house where he was given a few hours to rest his weary bones.

The great man was sleeping peacefully when just about dark, he heard the clop-clop of horses' hooves on the cobblestones outside the mansion. The Mayor's carriage was waiting to take him to the grand ball room. He arose from his bed, dressed quickly and was ushered to the dance at Demouy's Lafayette House on St. Michael Street. It was a gala affair and it would have been perfectly fitting and proper except that Lafayette didn't dance. Bred on the battlefield, the Marquis had never had time to master some of the social niceties. Instead, he sat on the sidelines and chatted with Noah Ludlow and some of the young ladies.

About ten o'clock, a visitor broke into the ball room and hollered, "Fire!" Most of the guests remained still glued in their shoes, but Lafayette was a man of action. Without a moment's hesitation, he ran to the window and jumped out, landing on St. Michael Street. When the crowds rushed to his aid, they found him unhurt and grinning. He had already figured out that a prankster was on the loose. The prankster was quickly given the boot and the band struck up another tune. The party broke up at midnight and Lafayette retired for the night.

The next morning, the Marquis was up early. The Mayor sent the carriage for him and together they rode over the city amid less furor than the previous day. After a stop at the Masonic lodge where Lafayette, a

Mason himself, autographed the lodge book, the mayor and the marquis drove on to the Garrow home for a spot of tea. Late that afternoon, Lafayette boarded a ship for New Orleans. In his farewell speech, he made an observation that no Mobilian would ever allow anyone to forget—"Mobile has the fairest women in America."

Today, Mobile treasures that statement and the Masons value the only Lafayette autograph in existence. The carriage that rolled Lafayette over the streets of Mobile was also treasured for a number of years but it was disintegrated in the great magazine explosion of 1865.

One of the Alabamians that had met Lafayette at Cahaba and had accompanied him to Mobile was the grandson of Ethan Allen. Henry Hitchcock had come to Mobile in 1816, got a job as Secretary of the Alabama Territory, then moved to Cahaba, and later had become attorney general. After Lafayette had gone, Hitchcock looked over the town a little closer and decided to stay. He had already made quite a name for himself as the author of the first book printed in Alabama. Now he was to begin a career that would establish him as one of the most influential men in Alabama's history. A lawyer by profession, he had earlier graduated to politician and judge. Then he got his hands in the contracting business and became Alabama's first millionaire. Dredging the Mobile harbor he started a boom in the port city that helped make Mobile one of the wealthiest cities in the nation. He joined the Presbyterian church but found there was no suitable church building. Hitchcock wasted little time in financing a magnificent church, for that day and age. Called the Government Street Presbyterian Church, it still stands today. In the summer of 1835, Hitchcock built sixteen brick buildings in downtown Mobile, giving the city its first "skyline." The next year he built the first public school in Alabama which today is known as Barton Academy.

But Henry Hitchcock was a perfectionist and a dreamer. He looked around the city at the mediocre hotels and rooming houses and decided that what Mobile needed was a fabulous hotel, one that would rival the luxuriant hotels of the East. He had laid the plans back in 1837, when he was still one of the wealthiest men in the nation. On Government Street just below Royal Street, he began construction of his dream building. Known far and wide as the Government Street Hotel, it attracted the curious from afar just to watch the construction. By early 1839, as the hotel was nearing completion, the English writer Buckingham visited Mobile and uttered a pronouncement that was music to Hitchcock's ears. "The Astor Hotel in New York will be second to none but this," said Buckingham. "This will be the greatest hotel in America."

But the year 1839 was a fateful one for Mobile as well as for Hitchcock. Just as his beloved Government Street Hotel was about to be completed, the old, dreaded scourge reared its satanic head. Yellow fever! One of the worst epidemics hit the city in 1839 and Henry Hitchcock was one of its first victims. The judge died with his dream clearly before his eyes, at the threshold of fulfillment. His hotel if not his body would live on as a lasting monument to his vigor and ingenuity. But unknown to Henry Hitchcock, forces had long been at work that would now come to a head in the latter part of that fateful year of 1839. For several years a motley crew had been meeting at a hide-away just outside Mobile, a place the Copeland Gang called "The Wigwam."

Chapter 9

The Unholy Three

The Wigwam was hot and crowded. The late summer air that pervaded the room was heavy with moisture that had driven many Mobilians out of the city and across the bay to rest in the cooling breezes that blew in from the Gulf. Before the mysterious group stood Gale Wages, a cunning, ruthless man who was in the act of initiating a new member into the clan. The new member was the son of a patriot who had fought with Andy Jackson years before in the defense of Mobile.

James Copeland, by name, the youngster had been born and reared on the Pascagoula River. Indicted for robbery by the State of Mississippi, he had been rescued by Wages when the clan leader helped him burn down the Jackson County Courthouse to destroy state's evidence. At Wages' invitation, Copeland came to the Wigwam to join the band of desperadoes that would one day live in folklore as "the Copeland Gang." James Copeland came before the group and Wages, assisted by his sidekick "Preacher" McGrath, inducted him into the clan.

The clan was no small operation. Over the years, Wages had molded a formidable organization which included some Mobile officials in very high places. Half of the Mobile police force belonged to the group. As soon as Copeland took the "blood oath," the clan spent the rest of the evening planning a grand assault to steal the city of Mobile blind.

It was an opportune moment for the clan to strike, that summer of 1839. Most of the wealthy merchants had departed the city to escape the yellow fever epidemic that was taking its toll during the simmering August days. A few nights later, just after seven o'clock, the clan slipped into the city. Each member was clad in his own separate disguise. Wages was sporting a long, handle-bar mustache, Copeland wore a cowboy outfit and McGrath was suited in the rags of a common beggar. Walking along Royal Street, Wages took a key from his chain and opened the front door of a jewelry store. Once inside, he signaled to his henchmen who then began hauling the loot to an old house near the old site of Fort Condé.

On a side street near Conti, "Preacher" McGrath picked a lock and broke in the rear entrance. Silently, as the moonlight cast a ghostly line of silhouettes on the sidewalks, the desperadoes lugged furs and antiques from the warehouse to the hide-out. From the cellar of the hideout, the clan lugged the stolen merchandise through a tunnel that ran to the riverfront where two large schooners were waiting. Stashing away the booty on ships, the men made another trip down the main drag, then another.

When Royal and Government Streets had been ransacked, the men sat down to rest in a back alley. Then Gale Wages looked at his watch. It was 11:45 P.M. In fifteen minutes a new shift of policemen would be coming on duty. The new policemen were not part of the plot and there was still work to be done. Racing down Royal Street the robbers tried a new trick. They set fire to a majestic building called "The Mansion House." This edifice was soon consumed in flames and the citizens came out to fight the fires that were spreading to other buildings. Volunteer firemen made a valiant effort to arrest the hot breath of the dragon that leaped across the alleys and ignited the whole block. Then the flames spread to the almost-completed Government Street Hotel and Mobilians watched in horror as the great building was enveloped by the fires. By one A.M. every soul in Mobile was at the scene, frantically trying to subdue the rampaging fire. Everyone, that is, except the arsonists. Over on the other side of Bienville Square, the clan was busy looting the remaining stores. Stealing across Government Street, the gang deposited their last haul by three o'clock that morning.

It was still dark when the two schooners sailed down the bay, but the sky was crackling with the sound of burning buildings. Wages and Copeland looked back at Mobile and saw a whole city in flames. They had put the finishing touches on the most disastrous summer in Mobile's history. Yellow fever had taken away nearly eight hundred citizens, including Henry Hitchcock, the city's chief financier and most prominent citizen. Now the fire had cost them their downtown section and most of the early French and Spanish buildings. While Mobilians were bemoaning their fate, the clan was busy burying its loot and money at a hide-out up Dog River ten miles from Mobile. All told, the takings amounted to twenty-five thousand dollars. After burying some of the gold and silver on Dog River, the clan members made a map, then quickly sailed out of the bay down to Pensacola to sell the stolen wares. They went to Galveston and New Orleans before they finally arrived back in Mobile the following year. Finding that the heat was still on, Copeland, Wages and McGrath buried about $5,000 at the Dog River refuge, then went west on a wild rampage that lasted several years. In Texas, they murdered two Mexicans; in Louisiana they poisoned an overseer and stole his slaves. On the Mississippi River, they hired an Irishman named O'Conner to float a barge down the river to New Orleans. Once they were down the river a bit, Copeland killed O'Conner, tied weights to his body and dumped him into the water.

Heading North through Ohio and Kentucky, the desperadoes left a bloody path as they ravaged and raped the land. When they finally returned to the "Wigwam" in Mobile, "The Unholy Three" found that a revolt had transpired within the clan—Gale Wages had been deposed as leader. James Copeland returned to the Pascagoula River, rounded up four of his brothers, Henry, Isom, Thomas and John and the reorganized clan declared war on the rebellious members. Harvey, the leader of the revolt, gathered up his members and fled to Perry County, Mississippi, with the clan hot on his tail. Outside of Augusta, a terrific gunbattle flared up and, when the smoke had cleared, Copeland found that Wages and McGrath were dead. Returning to Mobile, James Copeland was offered one thousand dollars by the father of the murdered Gale Wages to avenge his son's death. Taking the offer, Copeland led his gang back to Perry County.

On the night of July 15, 1848, Copeland entered the woods surrounding Harvey's house. The lamps were still burning brightly when one of Copeland's men was shot off his horse. Then the Harvey men blew out the lamps and the sound of rifle fire resounded through the forests.

Several of Copeland's men were killed but Copeland soon found Harvey, and shot him dead. Then the Copeland Gang retreated to Mobile, followed closely by the sheriff of Perry County.

Sheriff J. R. S. Pitts was a young man but he early found his purpose in life. It was to track down and capture the now legendary outlaw James Copeland. He notified the sheriff of Mobile County and the ring slowly began to close in on Copeland. It wasn't until the next year, however, that the manhunt had any real success.

Late one night, Copeland walked into a tavern near Dog River and got in a brawl with a man named Smith. Smith pulled out a small dagger and stabbed Copeland in the back. Copeland, alone and outmanned, fled into the swamps, painfully wounded. The tavernkeeper jumped on his horse and rode into Mobile to notify the sheriff of his suspicions that the wounded man might be James Copeland. The sheriff of Mobile County quickly brought in bloodhounds and they easily picked up the scent of Copeland's dripping blood. In the early morning hours the sheriff found Copeland in an old cabin on Dog River, too weak to run any further.

James Copeland served four years in the Alabama Penitentiary before being turned over to Sheriff Pitts of Perry County. He was speedily brought to trial and convicted of murder but the case was appealed and it was several years before the sentence was carried out. During these years, Copeland never gave up hope of being rescued by his brothers. Several attempts were made to break Copeland out but the most elaborate scheme involved the attempted bribery of Sheriff Pitts. The sheriff was approached by a certain doctor one day who offered him several thousand dollars to allow him to visit Copeland the morning of the execution. The doctor had hoped to slit Copeland's throat and to insert two small, iron bars on each side of the neckbone which would prevent his neck from being broken. His windpipe would be punctured, allowing him to breathe while he was hanging. When he was to be cut down, a reed would be placed in his throat which would stick up through the coffin. As soon as nightfall came, he would be dug up just in time to be revived. It was a wild scheme but Sheriff Pitts turned it down. Instead, the Sheriff kept a closer eye on Copeland by sitting at his cell door and writing down the last words of the condemned man.

On October 30, 1857, James Copeland walked to the gallows to face a huge crowd that had come from all over Mississippi and Alabama to watch him. Some had brought their picnic lunches and camped at the site all night and all day to be certain of a good seat for the hanging. Entire families had walked the distance from Mobile for the occasion.

At noon that cool autumn day, James Copeland walked up to the platform, made a public statement blaming his mother for his fate. She had been too good to him, he claimed, had always catered to his slightest whim. Then the blindfold was placed over his head as his last words soared over the audience. "Lord have mercy on me," he said, as the trap door slipped from under him.

James Copeland was dead but the story was far from over. He was carried across the river and buried on a steep bank. But not for long. Three nights later, his body was stolen and a legend began that Copeland had not really been guilty, that the Lord had resurrected him. Nevertheless, two years later, a doctor in Hattiesburg put on exhibition a skeleton he claimed was that of James Copeland. One day a man from Mobile offered the doctor five hundred dollars for it. The doctor refused but a few nights later the skeleton was found missing and was never seen again.

Meanwhile, Sheriff Pitts had been busy preparing a manuscript which he called, "The Confessions of James Copeland."

On publication, the book sold like wildfire until Pitts was sued for libel by two men who claimed never to have been a part of Copeland's Gang. Sheriff Pitts, vowing that Copeland had spelled out the names of every member of the clan, was convicted of libel and sent to the Mobile County Jail. The book was barred from further distribution.

Announcing he would republish the book, the ex-sheriff was finally released from jail and spent the next fifteen years dodging ex-members of the gang who did not wish to see their names in print. Miraculously, he escaped from several deathtraps and survived to publish a second edition. But as fast as the books came out, ex-clan members and relatives bought, stole and burned them. The book was republished again and again but even to the present day, it has a mysterious way of disappearing from local libraries.

The legend of the Copeland Gang looms larger with each passing year, mostly because of the lost treasures which today lie buried within the confines of Mobile County. In November, 1843, the clan buried a huge treasure in three wooden kegs somewhere in the Hamilton Creek Swamp but later removed part of it to Catahoula Bayou in Hancock County, Mississippi. Presumably, some of the treasure was buried in a cellar under the "Wigwam," but where was the "Wigwam?" A Mobile policeman thought he had found it in May, 1967, but the only treasure he was able to uncover was a gold-plated sword and some rusty chains. In recent years, an old map and what appears to be a coded message were unearthed by a resident of Pascagoula while digging for Indian artifacts in the neighborhood of Fowl River. But nobody has yet been able to put the pieces together and the legends go on and on.

Chapter 10

The Old Church Street Cemetery

South of Government Street behind the library building lies an old graveyard known as the Church Street Cemetery. The first of its inhabitants was laid to rest in the year 1819 but soon thereafter the cemetery received the unmarked bones of those early French and Spanish Mobilians who had been buried where the Cathedral Basilica of the Immaculate Conception now stands.

Upon entering the gates of the old cemetery, one is immediately struck by the variety of vaults, tombs and headstones that grace the quaint grounds. Most of the bones are housed in vaults, many of which are oven-shaped edifices of brick and cement. The smaller vaults are rectangular, covered by the flat marble slabs upon which the records of the deceased are inscribed. Then there are double-decked tombs containing two or more vaults, some of which are enclosed by low walls or by iron fences of ornamental design.

One sees the simplest types of tombs just after passing through the entrance to the cemetery. Near the front gate are the old tombs of the parents of Joe Cain, reviver of Mardi Gras. And right next to the parental tomb, lies the bright new tombstone of Joe Cain, himself. But Joe Cain did not always lie in the Church Street Cemetery. He died in the early years of the twentieth century and for over fifty years his bones lay in Bayou La Batre until the renowned folklorist Julian Lee Rayford led a drive to unearth and rebury them within sight of the famous Mardi Gras parades he had inspired.

Most of the tombs are in good condition but many of them show signs of age and neglect. Unvaulted graves are covered with masses of tangled vines, so thick as to hide the inscriptions on the stones. Perhaps the best preserved tomb is that of Don Miguel Eslava, treasurer to the King of Spain. This is doubtlessly due to the care given it by his descendants, the Douglas and Burke families of Mobile.

Moving further into the cemetery one comes upon the grave of Baron Jerome de Cluis, secretary to the Comte de Rivage, and his brilliant wife, Emilie, Marquise de Mezieres. De Cluis had been one of the Napoleon exiles who had come to Mobile after Waterloo.

Further on, we come to Louis, Marquis de Vaubercey, the last of the lords of Champagne, whose wife was Mary Elizabeth, daughter of Sir Robert Farmer, British Military Governor of Mobile.

Then we see the grave of Simon Chaudron, noted poet and literateur, who had been exiled with Napoleon to Elba, before escaping to Mobile.

One of the most intriguing of the plots is the so-called "Mother-Hubbard" lot. Many years ago this was one of those remarkable vaults which had rows of steps leading underground. Shelves for the coffins were on either side of the passageway. The story goes that an old lady was in the habit of walking down into the vault with food and a little oil lamp where she would remain for days at a time in that silent chamber for the dead. It was believed that she was in mourning for one of her loved ones who was buried on one of the shelves in the vault. A policeman who acted as a sort of night watchman used to keep a curious eye on her while she spent time in the vault. Late one night he became anxious, not having seen her for several days. Observing a glow coming from the entrance of the tomb, he crept to the door and peered in. The lamp was nearly burned out, the old lady had disappeared and was never seen again in Mobile.

Most of the events that have taken place in the graveyard have been somber, indeed. One thrilling incident, Mobilians would never forget. Early Sunday morning, May 11, 1834, a group of Mobilians were taking a stroll in the piney woods, just before the morning worship service was to begin. In a grove just south of the Church Street Cemetery, the strollers were aghast to see a pair of eyes staring up at them through a pile of leaves. Brushing aside the debris, one of the men recognized the body of Nathanial Frost, a young visitor to Mobile who only recently had come to the port city in search of work.

Police investigation turned up only one clue. A young man who had been seen in the company of the victim the night before was found to be missing from Mobile. Several witnesses reported having seen a certain Charles Boyington board a steamer heading upstream. Quickly, a posse was sent overland, on horseback, to try to head off the ship. On Monday, May 12, the posse arrested Boyington when the ship docked at Black's Bluff, before reaching Montgomery. Brought back to Mobile for questioning, Boyington disclaimed any knowledge of the death of Frost. Nevertheless, a trial began on November 16, 1834, and young Charles was charged with murder.

Charles Boyington was barely twenty when he went on trial for his life. A journeyman printer, a poet and an intellectual, he had been constantly in debt while in Mobile. However, when taken into custody he had nearly a hundred dollars in his wallet. Asked to account for the money, Boyington replied that he had won it by gambling but was vague about the details. He was equally hazy about other details in the case and could not even give a clear answer as to where he was traveling when apprehended. Witness after witness took the stand as the trial went into the second week. Perhaps the most crucial testimony came when the arresting officer told how Boyington, while still on the boat, took a metal object and flung it overboard. The officer surmised that this was undoubtedly the missing watch of Nathaniel Frost.

Despite Boyington's earnest denial of guilt, the jury brought forth, on November 29, a verdict of guilty. Boyington was sentenced to be hanged on February 20, 1835. The condemned man showed little emotion at the trial. It was a long way to the gallows, he reasoned. When he appealed the case to the State Supreme Court, Judge Henry Hitchcock, representing the Mobile District, was one of those dissenting. "As strong as the evidence is," the judge wrote, "it is all circumstantial." Nevertheless, the appeal was denied and Boyington went to his cell to await execution.

One day he was visited in his cell by the celebrated pastor of the Government Street Presbyterian Church, Dr. W. T. Hamilton. Dr. Hamilton had just come to

Mobile that very year. Born in England in 1796, his grandfather had been executed as a rebel in the Jacobite Rebellion of 1745. Emigrating to Mobile, he became pastor of the famous church that he was to head for the next twenty years. In his long career, Dr. Hamilton was never to undertake a duty that filled him with such pain as that which he assumed that day he walked into Charles Boyington's cell.

Boyington looked up at the minister and perhaps saw in his benign face a ray of hope. If he could convince Hamilton of his innocence, maybe the Pastor could procure for him a reprieve, a stay of execution or maybe even a pardon. It was worth a try, anyway. Throughout the long winter months, Hamilton spent hour upon hour talking with his pitiable young friend.

Hamilton, accepting the verdict of the court, was intent on convincing the prisoner that he must repent and ask forgiveness or risk eternal damnation. Boyington, however, not only denied his guilt but professed to be an atheist. Apparently, he hoped to enlist the support of the saddened minister by presenting a picture of a lost soul bound for hell unless his execution was prevented.

By February 20, 1835, Dr. Hamilton had grown to believe in the innocence of Boyington. Nevertheless, the good pastor had resigned himself to the carrying out of the court order.

Early that morning, the death march started out from the foot of Government Street. As the procession moved west the streets were lined with the curious and the bystanders saw something different in the manner of the procession. It was the custom of that day and age for the condemned man to ride to the gallows, seated on his coffin. However, the coffin was being rolled by a single horse, with Boyington walking close behind. Beside the prisoner walked his good friend, Dr. Hamilton, Bible in hand. Dressed in an ordinary black suit and a high, silk hat, Charles Boyington smiled confidently and waved to some of his friends. As the procession neared the grounds of the Church Street Cemetery, Boyington's eyes caught sight of the gallows and the smile slowly faded from his lips.

On the scaffold, he pulled out a slip of paper and began to read to the assembly. The sheriff listened for a while then yanked the paper from his hands. Boyington vehemently objected and began asking numerous, irrelevant questions. From the nature of his interrogation, it began to dawn on the sheriff that Boyington imagined that if he could delay the execution past the appointed hour, he could postpone the hanging. The sheriff asked Boyington if he had a last statement to make and the young man looked out over the crowd. "I am innocent," he cried. "But if I am hanged, a great oak tree will spring up from my breast so that this city will never forget the wrong it has done to an innocent man."

The crowd was as silent and still as the surrounding pines. Boyington looked for comfort but he found none. Then he looked to his last friend who stood beside him. Dr. Hamilton spoke to him in a whisper.

"In a few moments," he said, "You will stand before your God. What is your last declaration?"

Boyington looked at Dr. Hamilton and the color faded from his face as he realized that the minister was not, after all, going to make a last desperate appeal to the crowd.

"I am innocent," he gasped. "I am innocent but what can I do?" Dr. Hamilton turned his back and walked down the steps of the scaffold. Boyington looked back at the crowd. Terrified, he sprang from the platform. The guards swiftly latched hold of his arms and a mighty struggle ensued. Desperately, Boyington fought off his executioners, kicking, biting, screaming and cursing wildly. Finally, the guards caught hold of his feet and, clamping them together, lugged him back to the platform, where the blindfold was placed over his head and the rope around his neck. He was still kicking, crying and gasping for breath as the trap door gave way and his body fell down hard. The spectators were ashen-faced as they watched the body of Charles Boyington writhe and squirm on the end of the rope until its life force was gradually extinguished.

Then all was still. Grimly they cut down the corpse, laid it in the coffin and buried it near the northwest corner of the Church Street Cemetery close to the wall.

The people of Mobile tried to put the awful scene out of their minds but, like Dr. Hamilton, went on seeing visions of an oak tree which, to their horror, took root and began to grow on the spot where Charles Boyington was laid to rest in the year 1835.

Chapter 11

Madame Le Vert

Contemporaries called her "the most charming woman in the world." Washington Irving went even further. "She is," he said, "a woman such as appears but once in the course of an empire!"

Who was this wonder of Southern femininity who so completely captivated the imagination of men everywhere? Born in Augusta, Georgia, in 1810, she spent most of her early life in Florida under the name of Octavia Walton. Granddaughter of a signer of the Declaration of Independence and daughter of the Governor of Florida, the young Octavia had early become accustomed to mingling with the mighty and distinguished personages of her day. She quickly learned to handle herself with grace and dignity. Admiral Franklin Buchanan, who was destined to a rendezvous with the great lady many years later in Mobile, described her at seventeen, when she was entrancing the naval officers at Pensacola with an enthralling display of dancing and flirting. "Nothing,"

he said, "could exceed the brilliancy of her eyes or the
fascination of her smile. Dazzlingly beautiful, wherever she moves there is light in her path. . . .She is
encompassed by grace and splendor. . . .Rank, talent,
beauty—all contribute to aid the enchantment and
render the tenure of her powers secure. . . .She pos-
sesses in the highest perfection all the tender, graceful,
retiring attributes of woman. Being almost nature's
masterpiece, it is impossible to wish her different."

Was she really so beautiful? Perhaps not, but already, at seventeen, she had a way of making men think
so, a talent that was to reach fruition over the next few
decades. At twenty-three, she took a tour of the North
and succeeded in capturing the societies of Philadelphia,
New York and Washington. While in the midst of her
Northern campaign, Governor Walton came to Mobile
and began a law practice. When Octavia finished her
grand tour, she came to Mobile where the flower of her
personality was to reach full bloom.

Not quite a year passed before she found romance
under the oaks of the charming old city. It was a French
doctor named Henry S. Le Vert who, with a touch of
Gallic charm, wooed and won the flighty miss. Thus,
Octavia acquired the handle by which the world would
know her—Madame Le Vert.

The young couple built a fine home on Government
Street. There in the white and gold drawing room,
Madame Le Vert established the first American salon,
where dignitaries the world over would be entertained
for a quarter of a century. It was a lovely parlor, fashionable, charming and the Madame kept it open from
morning to midnight. She offered punch for the thirsty
and talk for the loquacious. Witty and refined, Madame
Le Vert entertained local politicians as well as noble-

men, ex-Presidents and artists. And all with equal gusto. Mobile society was the acme of the Ante-Bellum South and Madame Le Vert was Mobile society. No visitor to Mobile would dare fail to call on the great lady and no one who called would fail to receive a charming welcome. If the Ambassador from Spain paid a visit, he could expect some delightful conversation, for Madame spoke fluent Spanish, and when an Italian admiral docked his ships at the port of Mobile, he could always be assured of at least one listener. In time, Madame Le Vert mastered five languages. On more than one occasion, she was at the center of a five language conversation, interpreting the tongue of a Frenchmen for a nonplussed German and explaining to a local bumpkin the babblings of an Italian seaman. The interplay was sometimes amusing, sometimes serious but always vibrant. No wonder Madame was popular.

A reporter from New Orleans once visited the Le Vert salon and described it in the newspaper the next day. "From early starlight," he reported, "till the roses of morning began to lighten the eastern waters, the elegant mansion was a blaze of light in its drawing-rooms and halls. . . .illuminated with multitudes of many colored lamps in the form of fruits and flowers, shining as though an emerald veil had entangled swarms of fireflies, or flowers of flame and fruits of gold from fairy orchards were imprisoned within the clustering branches. About ten o'clock, the guests began to fill the spacious rooms, which were decorated with works of art and fine paintings brought from foreign lands. The walls of the principal drawing room, adorned by portraits of distinguished persons, were wreathed with garlands of the rich flowers then in luxuriant blossom; and in the midst of the roses stood the accomplished lady receiving her guests. What sculptured beauty in that rounded form!

She is not tall, but such perfect symmetry, such undulating grace, such decorous dignity, such cordial courtesy, such infinite adaptiveness of manner, you have never seen before. Her face is Madonna-like, brown waves of hair parting from a high, broad forehead; her eyes are blue and seem to melt with thought, and her chiseled lips are tinted like the delicate sea shell. She has made you think, just by her manner and her few felicitous words, that you are the very being she is most delighted to see. Such is the mysterious spell of her grace and courtesy. Look how yonder stairway is crowded! You may see the loveliness of Mobile gliding through the dance. The stars crowd upon each other. . . .All the elite of our city were present, many from the interior of Alabama, and some from New Orleans. Two thousand invitations had been issued, and the preparations for the entertainment were extensive. In our queen city of the Gulf there has never been a fete so magnificent."

One day the Madame received word that Henry Clay was on his way to Mobile. It was 1844 and the Kentuckian was generally considered to be a shoo-in for the Presidency come November. Certain he would not forget to call but taking no chances, Madame Le Vert rushed to the docks and personally escorted Mr. Clay up Government Street to her home. Later she sat next to him in the carriage while he was paraded down Royal Street. The crowds were raising quite a ruckus as the carriage rolled over Mobile, cheering the next President of the United States. Henry Clay, however, had his eyes and ears attuned to Madame Le Vert, apparently oblivious to the swell of commotion.

"Mister Clay," said Madame Le Vert, thinking to focus his attention to his admirers, "you are certainly loved in Mobile." The diplomatic Clay then demonstrated why he was such a successful politician. With his eyes still fixed on Octavia, he smiled and said, "No, Madame, it is for you that they cheer."

For twenty years Octavia's reputation spread far and wide, even to Europe where American society was usually belittled for its backwoodsy presumptuousness. Firmly established in America, she crossed the Atlantic for an audience with the Pope. Afterwards she went to Paris and was presented to Napoleon III at the Palace Royale by the mother of Empress Eugenie. Queen Victoria invited her to a ball, before she had even been formally presented to the royal family, a breach of royal custom that brought down criticism on the queen's brow. This was something that was simply not done, not even for the crowned heads of Europe. But Madame Le Vert was somehow different. For her all the rules must be broken.

Not everyone, however, would bend over backward for Madame. If popes and kings and queens were in awe of the Mobilian, there were some residents of Mobile who thought she was downright vain. Madame Le Vert wouldn't have denied it. In fact, it was a fault she helped to promulgate. In her own journal she unabashedly described herself in the third person, as if she were some historical figure. "All that she wanted," Octavia wrote, "she was given. In the intellectual and brilliant circles of other climes, she was gazed upon as a bright particular star from some sunny land. Crowds thronged around to flatter and to love. Rank, talent, wealth, all were laid at her feet. Triumphs were hers that even queens do not receive: 'twas the homage of the heart. The learned man paid his tribute of praise; the politician bowed before her. The old, the young, the grave, the gay—all joined in admiration of this one being."

Vanity? A touch, perhaps. No one doubted that "la grande dame" had ambition so no one should have been surprised. Ambition would be an impotent force without its being buttressed by a healthy dose of vanity. Besides, it was expected of her. Octavia was the southern belle of belles, the ideal par excellence, the great lady of Dixie. And the ideal southern belle was expected to be vain as well as vivacious; pampered as well as pretty. It was indelibly a part of her charm but it could not have been any other way. Years later, she confessed, in the third person, still, "Contradiction was never breathed to any of her words, while praise was lavished upon her every action. She was really deemed the eighth wonder of the world . . . the whole world seemed leagued to spoil her; parents, friends and lovers. Even while decked in her little white apron, lovers came thronging to her. Many were the tales of impassioned love poured into her childish and unheeding ears. She wept over the stories of some, and smiled at others. An unkind word had never reached her; she always had been told she was far, far above all others."

So went the legend of Madame Le Vert. Her long reign as Mobile's first lady stretched on through the Civil War but after that it came to a rather abrupt halt. La Madame became so wrapped up in entertaining all God's children before the war that she went right on with the indiscriminate catering after the war. However, Mobilians took a dim view of anybody, even Madame Le Vert, entertaining carpetbaggers. It wasn't too many punch bowls later that the once idolized Madame fell into sharp disfavor. She quickly surveyed her predicament and left Mobile for good, leaving behind her deceased husband and two daughters. She made a number of lecture tours over the country, describing her golden hours in Mobile and the people she had known all over the world. Finally, she went back to Augusta, Georgia, where she died in 1877.

In her time, Madame Le Vert had been a public idol, a social phenomenon of the times. And for somewhat inexplicable reasons. She had written no great book, had done no great deed, had been the wife of no great man. Her international fame must somehow have been due to the eternal compulsion of men to seize an idea, a dream, and nourish it until it flies away from reality to a pedestal all its own. And so Madame Octavia Le Vert reached the pedestal and became a cherished symbol of the ante-bellum southern belle.

She was still in her prime, however, when in 1861, Alabama seceded from the Union and the foreboding sounds of Ft. Sumter were heard from the East.

Chapter 12

Damn the Torpedoes!

Stephen A. Douglas sat in the office of the Mobile Register. Outside the building, on the streets, he could hear the chatter of tense Mobilians waiting for news of the Presidential election. There was excitement in the air but Douglas was solemn-faced. The parade was passing him by. People talked only of John Breckenridge and Abraham Lincoln.

In this, his last year of life, Douglas' thoughts went back a few years, back to the time he had introduced a bill in Congress called the Kansas-Nebraska Act which re-opened the slavery question. A lot of water had passed under the bridge since that year. "Popular Sovereignty" had not brought peace to the territories. Instead, it engendered "Bleeding Kansas," border ruffians and John Brown. A young frontier lawyer had risen to challenge the "Little Giant's" doctrine, but Douglas had slapped him down and won re-election to the United States Senate. Yet the frontier lawyer would not be put down for keeps.

Now, in 1861, Lincoln had captured the Republican
nomination with the platform of halting the growth of
slavery. Angry Southerners, convinced that slavery must
expand or perish, vowed to secede from the Union if
Lincoln were elected. Douglas, himself a candidate for
President, sat back in his seat and waited for the telegraph to click in the returns. Looking across the room
he could see his equally glum friend, John Forsyth,
seemingly lost in the act of reminiscing.

Forsyth, never optimistic, had even less reason to be
so on this occasion. His thoughts went back to 1835. He
was a twenty-three-year-old lawyer that year when he
first set foot in Mobile. His father, Secretary of State,
Minister to Spain and Governor of Georgia, had sent Forsyth to Princeton University in preparation for a political
career. In Mobile, John Forsyth was an immediate success. He practiced law, then was elected to the State
Legislature, then served as Mayor of Mobile. Taking over
the *Mobile Register,* he gained such national attention
for his editorials that he was appointed Minister to
Mexico.

Now, in 1860, Forsyth, perhaps sensing the end of an
era, ran his thoughts backwards, over the whole breadth
of his adult past, over a multitude of talented, exhilarat-
ing friends. He thought of the irrepressible Irishman
Theodore O'Hara, who had crashed into town in a wild
outburst of boasting and profanity. Wearing a stove-
pipe hat, O'Hara claimed he could drink anybody under
the table and tried to round up support for an expedition
to seize Cuba. Failing in this, he was appointed by Forsyth to take over the editorship of the *Register.* Wield-
ing a masterful pen, he carried in the *Register* one day
those immortal words which have since been carved on
the gates of the National Cemetery at Arlington:

"The muffled drum's sad roll has beat
    The soldier's last tattoo.
No more on life's parade shall meet
    The brave and daring few.
On fame's eternal camping ground
    Their silent tents are spread,
And glory guards with solemn round
    The bivouac of the dead."

Then there was Judge A. B. Meek, Alabama's first man of letters and founder of the public school system in Alabama. And Henry Hitchcock, Peter Hamilton, Madame Le Vert and Captain Foster. Foster, he remembered especially well because it was only the year before that the Captain and his boss, Tim Meaher, had been the central figures in a scheme that seemed to be a throwback to the swashbuckling days of the eighteenth century.

Meaher, it seems, was a gambler who also built schooners. On this particular wager, Meaher bet a huge sum of money that he could send one of his schooners to Africa and bring back a cargo of slaves to Mobile, right under the noses of Federal authorities!

Meaher put Captain Foster, his right-hand man, in charge of the expedition and one moonlit night, the fast schooner *Clotilde* was seen gliding out of Mobile Bay.

In the middle of the Atlantic Captain Foster found his compass going haywire. Finding himself way off course, he was caught in a hurricane which blew him to the Islands of Cape Verde. It was there that Foster found the source of his compass trouble. The chest of gold which he had hidden in the bulkhead was distracting his needle. The captain rehid his gold and got back on course but the price he had to pay was higher wages. The crew had spotted the gold when it was being trans-

ferred and demanded a raise in return for a promise not
to mutiny.

When the *Clotilde* docked in the Gulf of Guinea,
Captain Foster waded ashore and bought a hundred and
thirty Tarkars who had been captured from the interior
of Africa. Having never had a glimpse of the ocean, the
Tarkars went berserk at the sight of the rolling waves
and Captain Foster was forced to chain them all together
in a small enclosure.

Before the Captain had loaded the full amount of
slaves, he began to suspect that the slave traders were
also pirates. Leaving behind thirty-four slaves, he quickly
pulled anchor and set out to sea with pirate ships close
on his tail. Eluding the buccaneers, Captain Foster
sailed across the Atlantic and in less than a month
anchored off Dauphin Island. He left the slave ship anchored in Mississippi Sound and quietly sneaked into
Mobile where he found Tim Meaher anchored in a church
pew. Spotting Foster at the window, Meaher waited until
the offertory prayer, then sneaked out and the two enterprising gentlemen planned the final step of the expedition. A tugboat was sent to the slave ship and the *Clotilde*
was unmasted.

An hour before midnight, the *Clotilde* was being
tugged past the Guard House tower. The gong sounded
and the watchman called out, "Eleven o'clock and all's
well."

"So far, so good," Captain Foster retorted, under his
breath. The *Clotilde* made it to Twelve Mile Island up
the Mobile River and there the slaves were taken to a
nearby plantation. Tim Meaher had won his bet. However, the Federal agents were hot on his tail. Meaher
burned the *Clotilde* and later disavowed ownership of
the slaves, but it wasn't hard for the agents to figure out

that the slaves had just come from Africa, speaking no language but African, as they did. Unclaimed, they huddled themselves together at Magazine Point where they kept up their tribal customs and almost starved to death in a curious little community called Africa-town. But the Africans survived and many of their descendants still live in that neck of the woods which is today known as Plateau. The last of the immigrants died in 1945. "Uncle Cudjo," as he was called, preferred his African name of "Kazoola," and claimed that his life's ambition was to go back to Africa where his father was king.

As John Forsyth's thoughts drifted back into present realities, he and Stephen A. Douglas listened to the dah-dit-dah-dit of the telegraph as it tapped a foreboding message. After several hours, Stephen Douglas could read the message loud and clear. He would not be President; rather, it would be his hated adversary, Abe Lincoln.

Douglas must have felt a deep, personal loss but John Forsyth saw a bit more. Even then, he could peer into the next year and see Alabama leaving the Union. He must have shuddered as the nation crumbled and the Confederacy was formed at a convention in Montgomery. However, when the guns of Fort Sumter threw the states into mortal conflict, Forsyth, like his colleagues, resigned himself to the wave of enthusiasm that flooded Mobile. He even joined in it, like all those who, previous to South Carolina's action, were against secession. He was at the foot of Government Street when the crowds gathered around the "secession pole" to shout up the new flag and to sing the "Southern Marseillaise." John Forsyth was there for it all, for the long, wild and wooly succession of events.

A year later, Stephen Douglas was dead, but Forsyth was there to report Bull Run, Shiloh and Gettysburg. He was there to watch the city fathers prepare Mobile for its role as the last Southern city to surrender. He saw slaves cutting down the big oak trees to erect a barricade completely around Mobile. Then, secure in the belief that Mobile was impregnable, Forsyth went off to war as an aide to General Braxton Bragg.

Behind the lines of defense, Mobilians spent most of the war years gay and confident. General Joseph E. Johnston had said Mobile was "the best fortified city in the Confederacy." And even the Yankees had to agree. Fort Gaines and Fort Morgan at the mouth of the bay guarded entrance to the harbor. No Union ship would dare to pass those fearsome portals. But the Yankees set up a blockade out in the Gulf. If they could not get in, at least they would keep Southern ships from getting out. Over the next few years, the blockade tightened. Admiral Davy Farragut who was reared just outside Mobile captured New Orleans in 1862, then set up headquarters on Ship Island while he brooded over a plan to capture the city.

Meanwhile, Jefferson Davis came to Mobile. He looked over the defenses, made a speech and went to Richmond. Then he sent down a famous old war horse to take charge of the defense of Mobile. Admiral Franklin Buchanan had won fame as the commander of the *Merrimac*. After his battle with the Monitor, Buchanan came to Mobile and teamed up with General Dabney Maury to lay plans for the defense. Tough, experienced, and fiery, Buchanan had been chosen by Davis not only for his naval skill but because he had an intimate knowledge of the ways and methods of the cunning Admiral Farragut, having been a former classmate of his. As the war dragged on, Buchanan and Farragut eyed one another across the Gulf waters.

During the stalemate, Sherman marched his army to

Meridian from Memphis. From Meridian he was planning to attack Selma and then move down the river to invade Mobile. But his plans were thwarted by Nathan Bedford Forrest. Instead, Sherman turned toward Atlanta and began his famous march to the sea.

Across the bay General Grant had sent the survivors of the Vicksburg campaign. Under a flag of truce they were being cared for at the Grand Hotel at Point Clear. Grant's wounded were oblivious to a new contraption being built on the other side of the bay. Its designers were calling it a "submarine" but Buchanan was dubious of its value. The first one constructed sank but the second one blew up a coal barge in the Mobile River before it went to the bottom. Buchanan's interest was aroused but Mobile Bay was too shallow to put the underwater boat to any good use. The Admiral sent the contraption to Beauregard at Charleston where it sank the *Housatonic*. Mobilians were unaware that a new weapon had been invented under their very noses. They were still dancing and dining at Madame Le Vert's home when the most powerful iron clad ever built was towed down the Alabama River and into Dog River. The *Tennessee* had been built at Selma the year before. When the finishing touches were added, she steamed out across the bay, followed by three impotent wooden gunboats, the *Selma*, the *Morgan* and the *Gaines*. With these vessels, Admiral Buchanan went forth to defend Mobile Bay.

Looking through his binoculars, Admiral Farragut caught sight of the *Tennessee*. He had made up his mind to attack but when he saw the *Tennessee*, he held back. The magnificent ironclad appeared to be too formidable an opponent for Farragut's wooden fleet. Quickly, he asked Lincoln for some ironclads but the President was a long time replying.

While Farragut was waiting, an uneasy quiet settled over the city of Mobile. The ill wind bore increasingly bad tidings. Belle Boyd, staying at the Battle House, heard of the death of Stonewall Jackson. Then news came that Jeb Stuart had been shot off his horse at Yellow Tavern. Sherman had captured Atlanta and was burning his way to the sea. Lee was nearly surrounded at Richmond. But most depressing of all, news came that the great Mobilian, Admiral Raphael Semmes, had finally been trapped in the English Channel and the *Alabama* had been sunk. Could it really be so? The *Alabama* sunk? That most feared of all ships of the Confederacy, that ghostly galleon which had captured over seventy ships on the seven seas? Mobilians could hardly believe it. Some had halfway expected one morning, when the ring was closing in and Mobile was at her darkest hour, to look out over the horizon and see the banner of the savior ship sailing in at forty knots to rescue the lost city. As long as the *Alabama* sailed, there was hope. But now she lay at the bottom of the English Channel and a wave of gloom passed over the residents of Mobile as they somberly sipped at their coffee and nibbled at their grits.

They were rudely awakened on the morning of August 5, 1864. The big bell of the cathedral electrified the city! With quick, strong strokes the great gong sounded the alarm. The other bells over the city quickly followed suit and soon a nightmare of clangor brought the residents out of their homes and into the streets. They rushed to the edge of the bay, realizing full well that the long anticipated moment had arrived. Admiral Farragut had attacked!

Over the bay waters, the sounds of cannons rumbled across the waves. At the mouth of the bay, eighteen ships in a line, two by two, were moving straight forward, run-

ning the gauntlet between Forts Gaines and Morgan.
Only one stood out—*The Tecumseh.* Alone, unprotected,
she had fired the first shot of the battle. Now, within
range of the big guns of Fort Morgan, her captain spied
the *Tennessee* waiting patiently for her to break through
the narrow channel. The *Tecumseh* moved forward, her
crewmen anxious to be the first to attack the *Tennessee.*
But as the monitor *Tecumseh* was nearly past the fort,
a terrific explosion was heard. From Fort Morgan, the
Confederates could see the rear end of the *Tecumseh*
sticking up in the air with the propeller spinning furiously. A mine had exploded, sending huge clouds of
smoke into the sky. But had the mine only camouflaged
the catastrophe? Was it the guns of Fort Morgan or
those of the *Tennessee* which hurled the death blow?

The men on the deck of the *Brooklyn* let out a mighty
roar. The cheering soon spread to the *Chickasaw* and the
Metacomet. The Yankees thought that the *Tecumseh*
had sunk the *Tennessee!* When the smoke had cleared it
was believed that the Confederate torpedoes had sunk
the *Tecumseh* and the word was urgently delivered to Admiral Davy Farragut. The whole bay was laden with
mines. Would it not be suicide to send defenseless ships
against an invisible enemy?

Davy Farragut stood on the deck of the *Hartford,*
looking straight ahead. Nearing sixty years of age, he
was at the high water mark of a great career. Thus far,
he had made a brilliant record in the service of his
country. He had captured New Orleans and Biloxi and
had been instrumental in the capture of Vicksburg. His
reputation was secure. But if he blundered now, his
record might be permanently blemished. He might be
forever remembered as the buffoon who sent the greatest
naval fleet ever assembled to a needless death. Now he
must make a decision and he must do it quickly.

Looking ahead, Farragut saw the *Brooklyn* back-tracking, her engines reversed. In a moment, the *Brooklyn* would ram the *Hartford* and the whole fleet would be hopelessly entangled, sitting ducks before the mighty guns of Fort Morgan. Quickly, Farragut signaled the *Brooklyn*. "Why are you backing?" he demanded.

"Torpedoes in the channel," the *Brooklyn* signaled back.

"Damn the torpedoes! Go ahead!" he ordered. It was too late to back up now. There would either be a great victory or a disaster. The *Brooklyn* again reversed her engines and the procession continued up the channel, past the fort, into the bay. As each pair of ships entered the bay, Admiral Buchanan on the *Tennessee* tried to ram them two at a time. They were too fast but the guns of the *Tennessee* damaged ship after ship as they entered the bay waters. As each ship cleared, she began the pursuit of the three Confederate gunboats. The *Gaines* was run aground, the *Morgan* fled to Mobile and the *Selma* surrendered. There was nothing left now but the *Tennessee*.

The *Tennessee*, outnumbered seventeen to one, was still a formidable opponent. Buchanan, thinking he was unsinkable, began a furious assault on each ship. He was successfully ramming one after another. Then his eye fell upon the *Hartford*. He would destroy the *Hartford* and Farragut with it, if nothing else. Straight forward in the direction of the *Hartford*, Buchanan pushed the *Tennessee*.

Apparently, Admiral Farragut had the same idea. With the battle at a stalemate, he would send his *Hartford* against the mighty *Tennessee*. If he could gather enough steam, perhaps he could run over the *Tennessee* and if he sunk himself, he would, at least, take the

Tennessee down with him. Deliberately, the two captains steered their ships to a head-on collision as the great naval battle was coming to a climax.

Just when the two ships were upon each other, the *Tennessee* veered away and the *Hartford* bounced off her side and into an untenable position. The *Tennessee* let loose a volley of shell which tore through the *Hartford's* deck, killing and wounding a dozen men. The *Hartford* was then knocked into the path of the oncoming *Lackawanna* and a collision resulted in the *Hartford's* side being crushed. Farragut, thinking he was on the verge of sinking, rushed to the deck just in time to see the *Lackawanna* begin another charge at the *Tennessee.* Frantically, he ordered his signalman to wave the *Lackawanna* aside but the signalman became so excited he whopped Farragut over the head with a flagstaff.

By the time Farragut recovered, the *Chickasaw* had rammed the *Tennessee,* knocking over her smoke stack and stripping away her steering apparatus. After two hours of battling the deadliest armada ever assembled, Admiral Buchanan, with his leg broken and his ship hopelessly adrift on the bay, hoisted the white flag. The Battle of Mobile Bay was over.

The next day, Fort Gaines surrendered and two weeks later Fort Morgan gave up. But the city of Mobile held out for nine more months. Admiral Farragut, unable to move his ships in close enough to bombard the city, finally evacuated the bay and returned to Washington to become the first full admiral in the annals of the United States Navy. Admiral Buchanan was taken prisoner and sent to Pensacola while his comrades in Mobile barricaded the city and stacked all the cotton bales in Bienville Square. Robert E. Lee surrendered at Appomattox but Mobile still fought on. Then Blakely fell and the Confederates abandoned Mobile in hopes of joining

Nathan Bedford Forrest at Citronelle. When Union troops waded ashore, the Mayor of Mobile hopped on a carriage and rolled down the bay road to surrender the city to General Canby, waving a little white flag in the wind. Mobile, the last major city in the Confederacy, had at last fallen. A month later, news of Appomattox reached Forrest and he surrendered the last remnants of that once magnificent Confederate Army.

Chapter 13

The Incredible Carpetbagger

The morning of May 25, 1865 started out brightly enough. True, a touch of gloom hung over the city. Natural enough, since a war had just been lost. But Mobilians had already begun to get back on their feet. Just two weeks before, a group of prominent citizens had met at the Battle House and organized the First National Bank and there was talk of building a railroad to New Orleans. Never mind the flood of carpetbaggers and Union soldiers that were tainting the streets. Genteel ladies would step off the sidewalk rather than pass near them and the men could take care of themselves. It wasn't really all that bad. At least Mobile was better off than Atlanta or Richmond.

Over on Beauregard Street, the Federals established an ordnance depot in a warehouse and began to assemble military stores. Shells and powder were stacked up until a stock of nearly two hundred tons was on hand. Over the cobblestone streets, Negro workmen were rolling wheelbarrows full of live shells, singing and laughing as they worked. They were sweating more since their freedom than they did while they were in chains, but somehow they felt better about it. Several Mobilians, however, took one look at the explosives and hastened from the scene in alarm.

John Forsyth was in his newspaper office trying to meet a deadline when, just after dinner, he looked out the window and saw a cloud of black smoke rise into the air. Then he felt the building shake and the ground began to rumble. Huge flames shot up into the sky and the air was shattered by bursting shells. Two ships sank in the river; men were blown down in the streets and horses collapsed from concussion. Sidney Lanier, writing over at Point Clear across the bay, was startled by the blast. So were the soldiers down at Fort Morgan. They thought one of the monitors had struck a torpedo. The Battle House lost all its window panes and a man standing on the Church Street wharf was blown into the river.

A reporter for the *Mobile Morning News* rushed to the scene, describing the explosion as "a writhing giant-gaunt and grim, poised in mid-air. . . . bursting shells, flying timbers, bales of cotton, horses, men, women, and children co-mingled and mangled into one immense mass. The heart stood still, and the stoutest cheek paled as this rain of death fell from the sky and crash after crash foretold a more fearful fate yet impending; the lurid flames began to leap farther from the wreckage. Old and young, soldier and citizen vied with each other in deeds of daring to rescue the crumbled and imprisoned. . . ."

The fires burned until everything consumable had been destroyed. The entire northern part of the city lay in ruins. A great hole where the warehouse stood was later filled with water and remained a pond for many years.

The next day, Northern newspapers told how a vicious gang of Confederate officers—un-reconstructed rebels—had set off the charges even at the expense of their own people. Mobilians knew the truth, though. It had been plain carelessness by the military authorities that carried off the lives of three hundred innocent souls.

If reconstruction had been rather tame up to now, the great magazine explosion was just the thing to fan the flames of discord. U.S. District Judge Richard Busteed was shot by a local attorney named L.V.B. Martin in broad-open daylight, right in front of the Customs House on Royal Street. When the judge crumpled to the sidewalk, Martin walked up and shot him twice more for good measure. The nature of the dispute was never fully determined. The judge recovered, resigned and left town. Martin was never prosecuted and nothing much was ever said about it. It was just the feeling of the times.

Bishop Wilmer, the Episcopal Bishop of Alabama, had his troubles, too. During the war, he had altered the prayers of the church to include Jefferson Davis but to omit Abe Lincoln. After the war, he discontinued his prayer for Davis but refused to pray for Johnson or the United States as long as the military was in control in the South. "There is no civil government in the South to pray for" he argued, "and I can't expect my people to pray for a continuation of military rule."

The military authorities responded by closing all the Episcopal churches in Alabama and ordering the bishop to cease all religious activity. Bishop Wilmer, nevertheless, defied the orders and received nationwide applause. He held out against all threats of arrest, even a trial for treason, and appealed directly to President Johnson who was shamed into calling off his military dogs. Bishop Wilmer's victory was hailed as a spritely step in the direction of absolute separation of church and state.

There were many notable characters walking the streets of Mobile after the war. General Braxton Bragg came home and worked on the Mobile Ship Channel. Admiral Semmes opened a law office and General Beauregard was in and out of the city on business. Joe Cain dressed up like an Indian Chief and started Mardi Gras all up again in 1866.

But the most improbable character that ever set foot in Mobile appeared one day in Bienville Square the year after the war ended. Before he left Mobile for good, six years later, Colonel William d'Alton Mann would be a public idol, a living legend, the toast of the old town of Mobile. That day he arrived in Bienville Square, however, his prospects for public adulation could not have been dimmer had he been the Devil, himself. Even Satan rated more affection in those heated days of reconstruction than a carpetbagger. And carpetbagger was exactly what Colonel Mann was. To begin with, that is. A hero of the Battle of Gettysburg, he had led a cavalry charge against General Wade Hampton, then retired from the Union Army. Seeking to make a buck, he came South the year after the war ended. Years later, the Colonel explained, "I had always close to my heart a deep sympathy with the Southern people in their sufferings and deprivations. . . .The war over, my thoughts turned to the South, and I was so strongly moved by the conditions existing there that I determined to take the somewhat considerable means of which I was possessed—largely from royalties arising from my invention in army accoutrements—and go to the city of Mobile, cast my lot with its people, and do what in me lay toward its material . . . **upbuilding.**"

So the gallant Colonel found himself in Mobile, Alabama, but not before he had secured the hated position of Tax Assessor at the fat salary of $3,500 a year. The colonel could consider himself fortunate. It was not a bad intake for the year 1866. So what if he had to bear the whips and scorns of an abject neighborhood? But the colonel was ambitious. Not only did he covet more money, he wanted more power, more prestige and the satisfaction that he had helped his adopted community.

The colonel saw his first opportunity in the nearly defunct local newspapers. There were four of them in a city of forty thousand that could barely support one. The *Register and Advertiser,* the *Evening News,* the *Times* and the *Tribune* were all about to go under when the colonel rescued them with a minimum outlay of cash. Not too many months had passed before the colonel had bought them all out for a fair sum that helped retain for him the good will of the former owners. Combining the four plants, he then began to publish a single paper with a morning and evening edition, which he called *The Mobile Register.*

If Mobilians feared that the *Register* in the hands of the Federal Assessor of Internal Revenue would become an instrument of the Government, they soon were relieved of their misgivings. John Forsyth must have snickered in awe when it became apparent what the colonel was up to. A newspaper owned by a carpetbag tax collector becoming a rebel rallying cry? But the colonel knew when he had a good thing and he meant to use it. He attacked the local, state and national governments with equal gusto and spewed such venom on the carpetbaggers and ex-slaves that the *Mobile Register* became known throughout journalistic circles as the bastion of Southern resistence. He repeatedly editorialized, for the benefit of the local Negroes, on his theory of "the natural and indefeasible superiority of the white man . . . a supremacy that God has created." The irrepressible colonel even went so far as to attack Southerners whom he called "Scalawags." He was treading on sacred and dangerous ground when he, on one occasion, more than hinted at the misbehavior of General Beauregard, himself. John Forsyth must have experienced some inner convulsions at the thought of a carpetbagger Yankee was veteran, serving as Federal Tax Assessor in a southern city and using the hometown newspaper to attack the South's greatest living hero for scalawag inclinations.

The mere thought was unreal. But the redoubtable colonel was able to get away with it. Principally because he had other weapons than a newspaper. The tax assessing colonel was in a position to win as many friends as enemies. Particularly, rich friends. More particularly, rich Mobile businessmen who were willing to kick over a few thousand dollars in return for a few million in reduced assessments. The basic formula was simple; and what it equaled was money, power and social acceptability for the colonel. But the colonel even saw more to it than that. He saw it as a definite public service to the people of Mobile and boasted of millions of dollars he helped to keep in Alabama.

Now, with money and influence, the colonel turned his energies elsewhere. He persuaded the young Mark Twain to write a few pieces for the *Register*, for one thing. He had President Johnson's congressional message wired to the people of Mobile, for another. Then, he got a dandy of an idea. "In the reconstruction years," wrote the colonel many years later, "there was little for a Southerner to do but make things hot for the Northerners, hunt, fish, and run for Congress."

Run for Congress? Surely the colonel had flipped his

noodle, now. To win over practical, greedy businessmen was one thing but to offer himself to the man in the street, who was subject to all the prejudices that a foreigner could engender, was quite another. Or was it? The year was 1869. Two years before, Colonel Mann passed his severest initiation test and it endeared him to all un-reconstructed rebels.

It had happened in May of 1867 that a delegation of invaders from the North arrived in Mobile under leadership of Congressmen William "Pig Iron" Kelly, as he was known to Southerners because of the high tariff that he proposed on pig iron. The purpose of the Yankees was to instruct the populace on the Negroes' newly-acquired civil rights. Tongue in cheek, the Colonel admonished his readers not to become so overwrought by "Pig Iron's" lecture as to emulate Bostonians who had once torn a Boston Catholic apart in public.

"Pig Iron" Kelly then accosted Mann in his Battle House suite where he demanded to know the meaning of an editorial that appeared to suggest violence rather than prevent it. The colonel replied that he was rather proud of the subtle way in which he expressed himself in the article.

When Kelly rose to speak that evening he began to sense the effectiveness of Mann's editorial. His first clue came when a colleague to his right was shot dead on the platform. The second indication came when a colleague to his left fell dead. Leaping to the conclusion that a massacre was in the making, Kelly fell prostrate on the ground as the masses began to pounce upon the Yankee delegation. When the furor had passed, Kelly found that ten of his cohorts had been wounded but only one more had been killed. General Pope, the colonel's old commanding general, rescued Congressman

Kelly, then sent the survivors of the delegation back North. Pope's subsequent investigation claimed that Mann's inflamatory editorials had precipitated the violence and when Northern newspapers echoed the condemnation of Mann, the colonel got just the publicity he needed to foster his political ambitions. To the minds of Mobilians, the colonel had proved himself worthy.

In the summer of 1869, Colonel Mann was off and running for Congress. His opponent was another, more typical carpetbagger named Alfred Buck. Accompanied by his friends, Colonel Mann stumped the district with a band whose repertoire consisted solely of "Dixie" and a slogan that shouted, "Down with the Carpetbaggers!" All through the sweltering summer, the Colonel spread molasses over the gall, thanking God that he left the army before Sherman's march to the sea and swearing "to spend all the rest of my days in Alabama."

Three days prior to the election a Federal Treasury agent arrived in Mobile with the announcement that Mann was about to be arrested on grounds that he had misappropriated millions of dollars worth of Federal Revenue. This charge, of course, endeared him to his supporters and all Mobilians rallied to his defense.

By the time election day rolled round, riots had erupted all over Mobile, forcing President Grant to send in Federal troops to oversee the returns. Before midnight, the Mobile tally showed the colonel far out in front and the scattered returns from outlying portions of the district showed him in equally good position. The Democratic party called for a midnight victory celebration in the old Mammouth Hall. Amid the roar of the crowds and the rumble of cannons, Colonel Mann stepped forward and delivered a stirring acceptance speech. Following the oration, the cheering masses paraded down Government and Royal Streets celebrating the Democratic victory in a frenzied manner.

But two days later, when all the returns were verified, it appeared that Mann's opponent was the victor. The colonel's Confederate support had been overwhelming but the ex-soldiers, of course, had been dis-enfranchised.

The colonel struck back viciously in *The Register.* "Carpetbaggers, scalawags and hostile Negroes will finally be disposed of," he said. "We mean to meet force with force. We mean to kill. . . ."

Two nights later on the corner of Royal and Government, the Radicals held a ceremony in which they planned to burn the colonel in effigy. As soon as the figure was set on fire, a shot rang out and another full scale riot broke out. Three Negroes were killed and scores of others wounded before the troops moved in.

Although the colonel was forced to accept the electioneering defeat, he must have felt a certain smugness when the charges against him for fraud were quietly dropped. To the consternation of the Radicals, it seems that the colonel had, two years before, appointed his opponent, Alfred Buck, to the office of Deputy Tax Assessor, a post which Buck almost forgot he had held.

Defeat only spurred the colonel on. He threw a huge dinner at the Battle House attended by every important editor in the South. He invested a hundred grand in a cotton seed oil refinery which he called the Mobile Oil Company, the largest in existence anywhere. He promoted the mining of iron ore further up-state to such an extent that it would not be unreasonable to call him one of the founders of Birmingham.

Then he got into railroads. For several years the colonel had been advocating a railroad line between

Mobile and New Orleans. Now he got into the act, himself. He was elected a company officer, got the contract
for actually building the line and personally drove the
spike at the ceremony in November of 1869. Then he had
an even bolder idea. He would build a railroad from Mobile to the rich grain fields of Kansas and Nebraska with
a bridge across the Mississippi at Helena, Arkansas. The
result would make Mobile the greatest port in America.
He raised a hundred thousand dollars and got twenty-
four miles out of town before finances ran out. Then his
Mobile Oil Company burned to the ground and he lost a
small fortune trying to pave the soggy mire of Royal
Street.

After years of advocating Mobile as a town for tourists, the Colonel began to see himself as exactly that—a
tourist who had overstayed his fortune. So it was that
in the summer of 1872, Colonel William d'Alton Mann
left Mobile for another continent. He went to Europe
and consorted with kings and queens, all the while promoting his version of the luxurious Pullman car. His
Mobile friends followed his career closely for the next
forty years as he promoted a thousand enterprises all
over America, one of which was a subtle blackmail
magazine that he used to skin J. P. Morgan, Jay Gould
and the Vanderbilts out of untold thousands.

When he died in 1920, the Mobile Register's staff
still had not forgotten the legend that was bequeathed to
them a half-century before. "He was gifted with extraordinary vital force," so ran the editorial. "The Colonel
made himself one of the people of this city and state."

Chapter 14

Belles, Books and Pistols

The Federal troops were withdrawn from Mobile in 1877 when Grant went out of office. The cotton business picked up a bit and life around Mobile began to show some signs of its ante-bellum gaiety. The old names were gone, though. Admiral Semmes, Judge Campbell, John Forsyth and Madame Le Vert had all passed away, but there were some new ones to take their places.

Augusta Evans Wilson was another in a long line of remarkable Mobile women. As the darling of Mobile society, she had long been the heir apparent of Madame Le Vert. When finally, the Madame departed Mobile, Miss Augusta assumed the title of Mobile's first lady. She was already nationally famous by that time. "Miss Augusta," as she was fondly called by friends, had written a novel when she was only eighteen. In 1859, she published *Beulah,* a novel that gained a wide readership. Then the Civil War broke out. Augusta laid down her pen for a while and took up the nurse's uniform.

Sitting up with the sick and wounded Confederate soldiers one night, she began a novel that was to be called *Macaria*. All through the long nights she sat and wrote on scraps of wallpaper. When it was published under a Confederate copyright, the book was immediately banned by Yankee book dealers. This only spurred interest and copies were smuggled through the lines to the enemy soldiers. Eventually, it became as popular in the North as it was in Dixie. It was said that Confederate and Federal sentries sometimes made private truces while they pored over a copy of the book by firelight.

During the last year of the war, while Mobile was under siege, Augusta began the book that was to make her internationally famous. *St. Elmo* appeared in 1866 and she was immediately compared with Harriet Beecher Stowe. Two years later, she married the gallant ex-colonel L. M. Wilson and acquired an extra name for her books. For the next twenty-three years Augusta lived in blissful marriage. When the colonel died in 1891, she moved to a house on Government Street and kept up her writing. Critics said she wrote as if she had swallowed a dictionary but she paid them no heed. She kept turning out novels until her sixty-seventh year. However, it was *St. Elmo* that gained for her a lasting fame. Just west of Mobile, they even named a town for the book. Refined, reserved and beloved, Augusta Evans Wilson left a city in mourning when she passed from the scene in 1909.

Augusta had several noteworthy colleagues among the women folk. Madame Chaudron, daughter of one of the Vine and Olive colonists, published a number of textbooks for Southern school children. And Kate Cumming became the Florence Nightingale of the South, leaving her home to tend the wounded and dying Confederates on the battlegrounds over the South.

All of these Mobile women stayed around town, for the most part. But there were some who left the port city in search of more excitement. One of these was Alva Smith, daughter of William Forbes Smith, a wealthy old Mobile cotton merchant. Alva grew up in the old gray mansion on Government Street, went north and married William K. Vanderbilt. She soon persuaded Vandy to build a million dollar mansion on Fifth Avenue so she could snub the Astors. When the mansion was completed, Alva became the Queen of New York society, divorced Vanderbilt and went to Europe. Later, she became the chief financial backer of the woman's suffrage movement, then married her daughter Consuelo off to the Duke of Marlborough. The next year, Alva was welcomed at the Court of St. James to watch her granddaughter christened by the Archbishop of Canterbury. In 1962, the Mobile Historical Preservation Society wrote Consuelo in France and the Duchess responded with two old paintings, one of William K. Vanderbilt and the other of the former Alva Smith. Today the paintings hang in the halls of Oakleigh.

On August 8, 1889, Mobilians picked up the morning papers and thought they recognized a familiar name in the headlines. The world was to know her as Mrs. Maybrick but Mobilians remembered her as little Florence Chandler of Mobile. The daughter of the wealthy banker William G. Chandler, Florence had been born in Mobile in 1862. She later was sent to school in Europe where she met and married a wealthy English merchant named James Maybrick. After several years, Mr. Maybrick fell ill and Florence tended him during all the long days and nights of his illness. When he died, Florence was arrested and charged with murder. Thus began one of the most sensational trials in the history of English jurisprudence.

The prosecution claimed that Florence had fed Mr. Maybrick small doses of arsenic over a long period of time that eventually resulted in his demise. Defended by Sir Charles Russell, Florence claimed that the arsenic was planted in the house by Mr. Maybrick's kinsmen, in order to rob her of her inheritance. Technicalities in the case made it the topic of conversation of barristers as well as laymen and the appeals dragged on for years. Florence was sentenced to death, but the sentence was later commuted to life. She served fifteen years; then, without warning, was pardoned. Dozens of books and pamphlets were published dealing with the sensational trial. When Florence returned to America in 1904, she, herself, wrote a passionate, best-selling book on the case and her life in prison.

Sarah Bernhardt was a name that struck awe in the minds of people everywhere. When it was learned that the first actress of the world was coming to Mobile there was a mad dash to purchase every available theatre ticket. The great Bernhardt looked forward to making the trip over from New Orleans. The Mobile Theater had a fine reputation over the country; for half a century, the Mobile stage had hosted the best that Europe and America had to offer. The fabulous Jenny Lind had appeared as a child and later the original Joe Jefferson performed. When he died, his son, Joe Jefferson, Jr., hopped up on the stage and became America's most accomplished actor. Mobile theater-goers expected the best and they usually got it.

Most of the credit for the development of the theater in Mobile went to Noah Ludlow, an Easterner who had come to Mobile as a young man in 1825. He first built a theater on the corner of Royal and Theater Streets. Then he organized a troupe, went on the road, and came back in a few years to find that the theater had burned down.

Undismayed, Ludlow got some backers from New Orleans, built another one and left town again. Before it was over the theater burned down six times but it was always rebuilt and Noah Ludlow was usually at the bottom of it, when he wasn't in New Orleans or St. Louis.

When Sarah Bernhardt arrived in town, she was as anxious to appear on the renowned stage as Mobilians were to receive her. But there was a hitch to the contract. John McCullough, another celebrated thespian, was slated to appear on the stage several nights later. He had signed the contract with the provision that there would be no weekly performances before his own. This, he thought, would insure a certain "hunger" which would result in more ticket purchases. But surely the management would waive such an agreement to make room for the celebrated Sarah Bernhardt. Most anybody else would have, but not T.C. De Leon. De Leon, a versatile genius, exhibited a certain inflexibility when pressed to break a contract. He refused to allow Sarah to appear in the Mobile Theater but, always the man with a solution, he dreamed up an alternative: Sarah Bernhardt would appear in Temperance Hall!

When the prima donna walked into the place of performance, she looked around and saw an amazing sight. The stage was exactly twenty feet wide and twelve feet deep. The wall-paper was a hideous pattern of dominoes and the scenery looked as though it were painted by a juvenile. The curtain was nothing more than a flimsy collection of gunny sacks sewed together. To top it all, Sarah Bernhardt, accustomed to the most lavish dressing rooms in Europe, was expected to change in the corner with a thin white sheet separating her and the audience.

Poignant observers might have foreseen the eventual calamity had they noted carefully the manner in which

Sarah began to praise the set and surroundings. But the managers said nothing and hoped for the best. They were still hoping when the curtain went up for the first act and Sarah bounded on the stage, reciting her lines so fast the other performers were unable to keep up the pace. It was soon obvious to all but the most oblivious that the chafed actress was conducting the whole performance tongue-in-cheek. Still, the managers were hoping she would make it through the play. However, when the curtain went up for the third act, Sarah began acting up. At the banquet scene, she walked into the Duke's palace, flopped down at the table, picked up a drumstick and began beating it on the table with such ferocity that the table fell in. Then she took a chunk of chicken and flung it out into the audience. When the audience gasped, Sarah broke into a fit of giggling. Then she began screaming her lines. Professor Schlesinger, conducting the orchestra, signaled to his musicians to up the volume. This only increased Sarah's wrath and she began to scream even louder, which made the orchestra hit a triple forte to cover up for her. And Sarah and the band played on.

When Temperance Hall had nearly burst wide open, the frustrated actress let out one blood-curdling scream and then ran back to her corner behind the sheets. The curtain, such as it was, rang down and the managers shortly appeared, announcing that, due to illness, the show could not go on. A few patrons walked to the box office and demanded a refund but most Mobilians felt that they had gotten more than their money's worth. They had been handed the rare privilege of seeing the legendary Sarah Bernhardt in the midst of one of her celebrated tantrums.

It wasn't the only time Mobile theater-goers got more than their money's worth. Some of those in Temperance

Hall that night could remember back to the night of March 25, 1842. At that evening's performance, another actress, Miss Hamblin by name, got heated up, too. She didn't just scream, though. At an opportune point in the performance, Miss Hamblin added considerably to the flow of drama by taking a dagger and gigging her husband, the leading man. As he lay dying, Dr. Henry S. Le Vert leaped upon the stage and Miss Hamblin hopped out the window. Edward Ewing, the actor, died almost immediately and a frantic search for the murderess began. It was several months later before she was found hiding in a closet in the home of a friend on Jackson Street. Speedily brought to trial and charged with murder, she was finally acquitted when Dr. Le Vert testified that the victim may have died of a seizure before he bled to death. The results of the trial were heatedly contested by the local citizenry but Miss Hamblin didn't waste time arguing with anyone. As soon as she hit the door, she took off for New Orleans and spent the rest of her life portraying characters with a little less realism.

A few years after this bit of drama a select group of Mobilians were privileged to witness one of the last of the old-time duels. One spring evening in the year 1859, two men met under an oak tree in a vacant lot at the corner of Augusta and Scott Streets. They had just come from New Orleans where they had accidentally met in a poolroom in the Vieux Carré. A few months before that, one of the men, James Stith by name, had stomped away from a garden party in Vicksburg, Mississippi, insulted by his friend Henry Vick.

Henry Vick was a brash young man, impetuous, bold, even reckless. A nephew of the founder of Vicksburg, he was both arrogant and proud when he felt his honor had been impugned. And anybody who stomped away from his party had certainly impugned his honor.

With his wedding less than a week away, Vick went to New Orleans to purchase some wedding gifts and items to be used on the occasion. After making the purchases, he walked into the poolroom one night and found Stith huddled over the bar. Seeking to needle his erstwhile friend, Vick announced that he was buying everybody in the house a drink. Stith turned and snarled. "I drink only with gentlemen," he said.

"I am a gentleman," retorted Vick. "But I retract my offer. Instead of a drink, I challenge you to defend your honor."

Stith was obliging and the arrangements were made by the contestants' seconds. Dueling had by that day and age been made illegal, so off the party went to Mobile where it was thought the ban was not so rigidly enforced.

It was a foggy evening in May when the two combatants faced each other under the oaks of old Mobile. Back to back, Vick and Stith walked away from one another, armed with Kentucky rifles. At the end of fifteen paces, they turned and aimed. Vick, the more adroit sharp-shooter, shot first. His bullet just grazed the top of Stith's hairline as Stith pulled his trigger. Stith had aimed at his adversary's heart but the bullet ripped down Vick's gun barrel and shattered his forehead. Vick crumbled to the ground, bereft of life.

Out from the shadows stepped Dr. Lawrence A. McClesky. He and a few fellow Mobilians had been watching from the bushes. Finding Vick dead, Dr. McClesky sent the body to the morgue and offered his home to the dead man's seconds. Stith and his two companions fled to the waterfront and hopped the mailboat sailing back to New Orleans.

A. G. Dickinson, one of Vick's seconds, was a close personal friend of Vick. He was safe in Dr. McClesky's home but he couldn't bear to think of his friend Vick lying in a cold morgue with his fiance waiting patiently in Vicksburg for the wedding that was to take place in two days. Leaving his refuge, he went to Police Captain Harry Maury and made a full confession. Maury was touched and agreed to help Dickinson get Vick's body out of town before his fellow policemen tracked them down. The sympathetic Captain Maury put them both on a ship and locked them in the ladies' restroom. Just as the vessel was to leave Mobile, the police stormed aboard and were about to investigate the restroom when the captain stopped them. "Nothing but two old ladies in there," said Maury. "They became terrified when they saw us boarding the ship." The ship pulled safely away and Captain Maury was satisfied that he had done his good deed for the day, albeit at the expense of the law.

Dickinson reached New Orleans just in time to board the steamer heading up-river. Two days later, the body of Henry Vick arrived in Vicksburg. The dead man lay peacefully near the boxes of wedding gifts he had purchased for his bride. Then Dickinson went about the sad task of informing the bride-to-be that there was to be a funeral instead of a wedding.

Two years later James Stith joined the Confederate Army. He was immediately sent to Vicksburg where, in 1863, he died in the siege of that city and was buried within a stone's throw of the friend he had killed in the Mobile duel.

Chapter 15

John Fowler Turns the Century

As the Twentieth Century came into focus Mobilians wavered between reflecting on the past and looking toward the dawn of a new era. Things were really changing fast. It was only a few years before that Oscar Wilde had sauntered into town and shook everybody up with his new-fangled ways. This was in 1882 and Mobilians just weren't prepared for that beatnick whose long hair and strange clothes and ideas on aestheticism seemed way-out. Oscar ambled on stage at Frascatti's summer theater the night of June 28 and alarmed many of his listeners. He wasn't able to change many minds but he painted a glowing picture of the future which helped prepare Mobilians for the changing times.

And times were changing fast. Not only culturally and socially but in several other fields. Inventions especially were catching America's eye; the light bulb really turned Mobile on. In 1879, the city got its first telephone and a few years later saw its first horseless carriage. Into the full limelight of these years stepped three progressive gentlemen. One was to transform a city, one was to affect a world and the other was branded a crackpot.

The man who transformed the city of Mobile was known affectionately as Captain Pat Lyons. His parents had emigrated to Mobile in 1849 where Pat was born six years later. Growing up on the river, he rapidly took to the water and became a deck boy on the river steamers. He showed so much energy and capacity for leadership that the deck hands began calling him "Captain Pat." When he grew up, Captain Pat left the river and got into the wholesale grocery firm of Michael and Lyons. As a merchant, he was an immediate success. He was soon a director of several corporations and was appointed vice-president of the City Bank and Trust Company.

Then Captain Pat got into politics. In 1897, he was elected to the City Council and became the most influential member of that select group. By 1904, he had so distinguished himself that he was elected Mayor of Mobile. Now he could really go to work.

The city had a floating debt of $150,000. Within a few months after taking office, Mayor Lyons miraculously paid off the debt and the city had a surplus on hand. Then the Mayor looked around and saw that the city streets were slightly dusty so he began a huge program of paving. Then he redeemed the city's wharf property which had been heavily mortgaged. He lowered the city taxes and started the drive for a city water works. Besides being a good manager, Captain Lyons had a keen eye for beauty and what it might do for tourism. He started the planting of azaleas in Bienville Square. The famous purple azalea plant so long admired by tourist and resident alike was planted by the Mayor, himself.

He improved Washington Square, then built several playgrounds and recreation areas. His efforts were not lost on the voters. They re-elected him mayor in 1911 and again in 1915. It was after World War I that Captain Pat finally retired and when he did, the city of Mobile named a park after him in appreciation. All the city, young and old alike, loved Captain Pat. Scores of little children called him papa, even though they had never met him personally.

In 1897, Mobile was visited for the last time by its old nemesis—yellow fever. Down through the years, the dreaded disease had been the scourge of the city. Who could ever forget the epidemics of 1704, 1819, 1839, 1853 and 1878. The epidemic of 1878 had been the last one contemporary Mobilians could clearly remember. They remembered Father Ryan, the poet-priest of the Confederacy, whose heroic work during that year endeared him to nearly every family in Mobile. When it was over and the disease had taken its awful toll, Mobilians uneasily awaited its return. For the epidemic was certain to return, sooner or later. Despite all the advances science had made in the several decades after the Civil War, yellow fever remained a mystery, an inexplicable deadly riddle, beyond the reach of human understanding. Or so it seemed to most people. But even as the cries of "Yellow Fever" were heard on the streets of Mobile in 1897, a young doctor from the port city was hot on the trail of the villain.

William Crawford Gorgas had been born in Toulminville in 1854. After graduating from medical school, Gorgas found many lucrative fields open to him. But he knew what he was after. All his life he had heard the pathetic tales of yellow fever epidemics. With his own eyes he had seen the fever come and grab hold of men. First the high fever, then a racking cough, a sinking pulse, a reddening of the skin, a bluing of the eyes, followed by convulsions; then finally, the fatal black vomit. All his life, William Gorgas had watched helplessly as his neighbors and kinsmen were seized by the disease. Now, as a young doctor he was determined to do something about it. He thought he knew the answer but it wasn't exactly his own idea. As a young student he was markedly influenced by a great physician, Dr. Josiah Nott. Dr. Nott had helped form the Mobile Medical Society in 1841. Just before the Civil War, he was one of the founders of the Medical College of Alabama in Mobile. Four of his eight children died of yellow fever and Dr. Nott thereafter devoted most of his energies to seeking the cause of the fever. He even had a theory that yellow fever was transmitted by an insect; a mosquito, maybe.

Few people paid much attention to Dr. Nott's theories. But William Crawford Gorgas remembered his work and years later, after Dr. Nott had passed on, Gorgas took up the task. After medical school he joined the army and became a military doctor. At Fort Brown, Texas, he caught yellow fever and developed such an immunity that he was sent to several stricken areas. More and more he came to believe that the mosquito was the villain. When Walter Reed finished his famous experiments, Gorgas put the newly acquired knowledge to work. He sailed to Havana and went to work on a ravenous epidemic that had already been in progress for several weeks. Attacking the low, swampy areas and breeding grounds, Gorgas wiped out the fever in a few months and rid Havana permanently of yellow fever.

Gorgas' work in Cuba brought him international fame as a sanitarian. When Teddy Roosevelt set the dirt to flying in Panama, he picked Gorgas to stamp out yellow fever and pave the way for the success of the canal.

It was yellow fever that, more than anything else, stopped the Frenchman deLesseps in his gallant attempt to sever the hemisphere. The Americans, however, were successful and a lion's share of the credit went to the man from Toulminville, William Crawford Gorgas. He was hailed by presidents, feted by kings. George V of England knighted him just before Gorgas died in London in 1920. Perhaps his greatest honor was that of being the only native-born Alabamian to be elected to the American Hall of Fame.

About the time Dr. Gorgas was perfecting his sanitation program, Mobilians were saddened by several catastrophes. Besides the fatalities of the 1897 epidemic and the Spanish-American War, there was the *S.S. Mobile*. A British steamship, *The Mobile* had been fervently welcomed into port just before Christmas. On December 28, 1900, she sailed out of the bay with 28 men aboard and was never seen or heard from again.

Then there was poor old Matt Sloan, Mobile's first fire chief. For two decades, he bravely defended the city from the fires which devastated Mobile. He was still fighting them when the alarm sounded on October 11, 1901. Chief Sloan jumped into his horse-drawn fire wagon and raced to the scene of the blaze. To speed the wagon on, he jumped out and was running behind the horses when he keeled over and died of a heart attack at the corner of Government and Saint Emanuel Streets.

Across the bay, residents of Baldwin County were in a frenzy. In 1893, a Negro named Morris Slater had walked into a little town near the Escambia County line, toting a rifle on his broad shoulders.

"Gimme that gun," said the first policeman that passed him.

"Nawsuh," said Slater. "It's my gun. I got a license."

"You gimme that gun or there'll be a dead man lying
ing here," said the policeman.

The policeman was right. A brief scuffle followed,
the gun went off and the man in blue fell dead. Morris
Slater jumped on the north bound freight train that was
pulling out and rode into everlasting fame. When he
hopped off further up track, he was already known far
and wide as "Railroad Bill."

Over the next few years, "Railroad Bill" stirred the
imagination of the darkies between Flomaton and Bay
Minette. He would hop on the freight trains passing
through Baldwin County and rob the cars of their food
and supplies. He slept by day and rambled by night.
Posses were formed all over South Alabama in hopes of
tracking down "Railroad Bill." But they couldn't catch
him. The Negroes in the area said nobody could catch
"Railroad Bill." He was a black chameleon who could, on
a moment's notice, change into a fox, a chicken or a cow.
It was only when he was cornered and had no time to
change that he used his rifle. As the years passed, the
ring began to close and "Railroad Bill" was forced to
use his rifle more often. The number of his victims went
to the dozen mark, a fact which catapulted Bill into the
political limelight. To be elected, a sheriff had to swear
he would be the one to get "Railroad Bill."

Sheriff E. S. McMillan was one of the candidates
elected to office on that platform. On a hot July night in
the summer of 1895, the sheriff took his son and a
doctor and hit the trail. Several hours later, he came
upon what appeared to be a deserted house.

"Who's there?" a voice called out. Then a shot was
fired. The intrepid sheriff walked out from behind a
tree and was in the act of raising his gun when he was
shot through the heart. The doctor ran quickly to his
side and asked if he were hurt.

"Yes," said the sheriff, "I'm killed." Victim number thirteen was carted to the burial ground and "Railroad Bill" became an even grander figure; a folklore hero, a god of the black man. From out of the big woods a song was on the darkies' lips:

"Railroad Bill, Railroad Bill
Never been caught and he never will
Railroad Bill . . ."

Over the next few months the specter loomed larger. A special posse was sent out on a train. They would be the ones to get ol' Bill. But the black phantom hopped the very train they were riding and robbed it of its valuables right under the noses of the posse. A farmer ran into his chicken yard one night and shot a giggling trespasser but it turned out to be a possum, instead. "Railroad Bill" was running wild over the countryside, changing into a beagle hound, then back into a Negro, then into a fox. The Negroes said he would never be caught and they believed it.

Early one morning in the Spring of 1896, a disheveled colored man walked into Tidmore's store just outside of Atmore. He ambled up to the counter and was reaching for the money box when a deputy named R. C. Hohn stood up and shot him in the side. The black man teetered and fell toward the door as another deputy stepped up with a shotgun and blew his head half off. Sheriff McMillan, brother to the murdered sheriff, then burst into the store and identified the dead man as Morris Slater. The two deputies shared the reward while the sheriff settled for the body. He exhibited the corpse in every town from Bay Minette to Brewton, using it as an example of the wages of outlawry.

White men were surely convinced but the Negroes only laughed. "Dat ain't no Railroad Bill," they would say. "Why, Railroad Bill, he out dere grazin' in de pasture, somewhere, jest a-laughin' at all you foolish policemans."

"Railroad Bill" was a legend in Baldwin County. About the same time he was wreaking havoc across the bay, another legend was winding up his last days just north of Mobile at Mount Vernon. He was famous in England as "Jerome," but Mexicans had Latinized his handle and the world knew him as Geronimo, the wild Apache Chief who terrorized the United States Cavalry. Geronimo was finally captured in 1886. Imprisoned for a while in Arizona, he was then sent to Fort Pickens in Pensacola. On his way to prison, his train stopped at the Mobile depot where several thousand Mobilians gathered to get a glimpse of the old warrior. But the crowd was somewhat disappointed when Geronimo only stuck his head out the window and glared.

Several months later, though, Geronimo was back in Mobile. The climate at Fort Pickens was not so healthy for the Apaches and the Government was transferring them to Mount Vernon. Geronimo and his braves camped out in the hills around Mount Vernon for several years, living much as they did back in Arizona. Geronimo made a fat living by signing autographs for a dollar a signature and posing for pictures. In 1894, his son Crappo died and Geronimo journeyed to Mobile with his two wives for the burial rites.

There were other characters around Mobile, too. Cleveland Prichard had purchased some land in 1879 just west of Magazine Point. He made arrangements with the Mobile and Ohio Railroad to build a depot there and before long, had a thriving business. He opened up the community as a vegetable center, named the settlement after himself, and soon became known as the "Vegetable

King of America." Then he built a racing track where downtown Prichard now stands which brought in famous horses from all over the world.

Then there was "Whistlin' Bill" Nichols who came to Mobile and started a fad. It really began as a New Year's Eve celebration. "Whistlin' Bill" would blow his boat whistle every year on that occasion for several hours at a time. He liked the way it sounded so much he took to blowing it for other occasions. Then it became a daily event. He even learned to play tunes on his whistle. It soon happened that other Mobilians began to horn in on his act. Finally, the fad swung into full force. Every evening when Bill sounded his horn, hundreds of Mobilians took up their horns and whistles and joined him. They were all having a fine time driving the residents to distraction when City Hall got in on the show.

The *Morning Register* of January 31, 1912, carried a dismal decree from the city government. "No steam whistle," the ordinance read, "shall be blown in the city of Mobile between the hours of 8:00 p.m. and 6:00 a.m. for a period longer than ten seconds. Violation shall be punished by a fine of not less than $5 nor more than $100."

"Whistlin' Bill" goodnaturedly retired from the show, except for New Year's Eve when he cut loose with two renditions that his listeners vaguely described as "Old Black Joe" and "Carry Me Back to Old Virginny."

The most fabulous character of all was the irrepressible John Fowler. John made his living as a clock maker but that was just a sideline. Most of his time, he spent preaching, advocating social reforms and building airplanes.

"Fifty dollars a day for every working man is perfectly reasonable," he would say. "But workers should be paid with 'time checks' instead of cash." Mobilians might have called him a communist but nobody knew what that meant in 1900.

Brother John would take his soap box all over town and preach a sermon at the passing of a hat. But his favorite place was down at the waterfront where he harangued his listeners on the folly of sin. "The greatest sin," he said, "is not thinking-mental laziness."

One Saturday evening on the waterfront, one of the irreverent members of his congregation had the audacity to pipe in on his sermon. It was in the summer of 1892.

"Well," said the questioner, "What have you been thinking about?"

"I've been thinking about an airplane," retorted John. "Not only that, I've already built one and I'm working on another."

Murmuring in the congregation indicated that there were some "Doubting Thomases" among his listeners. "Tell you what," said Brother John. "With the Lord's help, I'll be finished with my new machine in three weeks and I'll fly it across Mobile Bay."

The sermon abruptly ended and the people departed shaking their heads. But true to his word, John Fowler completed his new machine in three weeks. On a Sunday afternoon on the beach of Monroe Park, John Fowler and a little colored newspaper boy named Charles Jackson stepped in his airplane and rolled down the runway.

Thousands of curious Mobilians lined the beaches that afternoon. It was a bright day with a brisk wind blowing so hard it almost reached hurricane velocity. The bystanders were utterly incredulous as they watched the buzzard-like contraption take off.

"We come rolling down the runway," said Charles Jackson, years later, "and the wind just grabbed us up. I was running the propeller and Mr. Fowler was doing the guiding. We floated up and out across the bay like a feather but Mr. Fowler saw we couldn't make it to the other side, we was gone two or three miles, and he turned us around. We went sailing back to land and crashed into the sand and broke the wheels off the airplane."

John Fowler never got national credit for the first airplane flight but maybe he should have. He got quite a lot of local recognition, though, and his plane was put on exhibit. Several Mobilians swore they saw the Wright brothers looking at the strange contraption in 1900, three years before they made their historical flight. But fame or not, John Fowler went on making more airplanes. One of them, he showed to a friend of his known as Professor O. E. Williams. The Professor built one himself, very similar to Fowler's. Then he took it on a tour through the mid-west giving demonstration rides. His grand exhibition was at the Gulf State Fair in Mobile on October 17, 1917, when he went up for a spin, then crashed, and died in Mobile Infirmary.

But John Fowler was not discouraged by the Professor's catastrophe. He built another airplane that very year. In 1925, he built his last flying machine. This plane was a little different. It had a motor and was designed to fly straight up, like an autogyro. This one didn't succeed, but it became the forerunner of what later would be known as the "helicopter."

John Fowler lived to be 77. Before he died in 1939, he went through a long period of illness and was confined to his Dauphin Street home. A few days before he died, he got up from his bed and walked down to the riverfront where he preached his last sermon. His theme was the same: "Be active, do some thinking and don't waste time."

One of Brother John's proudest moments came from practicing just what he preached. When the hurricane of 1916 struck Mobile, the old clock on top of the county court house was severely damaged by the wind and water. It was a beloved old clock and the city officials wished to save it. They paid a goodly sum of money to get one of America's foremost clock repairmen from New York to come to Mobile and work on it. After a few days, the distraught Yankee gave up and went back North. The clock was hopelessly mangled and waterlogged. John Fowler heard about it, volunteered his services and took to the task. It was meticulous work and well-nigh impossible but Brother John worked on it "round the clock" and in the space of a few days, had it running good as new. The clock was used for many years after that time but nobody ever suggested calling anybody in from New York as long as John Fowler was around.

Chapter 16

Woodrow Wilson at The Battle House

At 10:45 p.m. on the night of February 12, 1905, one of the cooks came rushing out of the Battle House Kitchen. "Something's on fire upstairs," she yelled. "I can hear something burning."

When black curls of smoke came rushing down into the kitchen, there was little doubt that an advanced fire was sweeping the building. Steward A. E. Reynolds rushed to the annunciator system and calmly announced to the 147 guests that the Battle House was burning. The patrons grabbed what belongings they could and quickly filed out of the hotel as the Mobile Fire Department rushed up to battle the blaze. Ten leads of hose were dragged into the building, ladders were strung up and the water began to spew from the nozzles. Within an hour, thousands of Mobilians surrounded the famed old hotel to watch it crackle and burn. Just after midnight, the roof fell in, cutting off power and communications in the downtown section. Within another hour, everybody knew it was a lost cause. The floors began to topple, one after another until there was nothing left but a mass of bricks and mortar and twisted iron rods. The old Battle House belonged to the past.

The famed hotel had first opened in the year 1851 when the Battle Brothers, James and Samuel, had organized a company to build something to take the place of the new Mansion House, which had burned the previous year. The old Mansion House had burned back in 1839, along with the Government Street Hotel, and Mobile, famed for receiving her visitors in luxurious fashion, had nothing to offer travelers. But in 1851, on the site where Andrew Jackson had once set up his headquarters, the construction of the Battle House was begun. On November 13 of the following year, it was completed and opened its doors to visitors.

The Battle House had many guests over the years and it made a keen impression on all of them. What it lacked in size, it made up in good Southern hospitality. Everybody who stayed there went away satisfied. Amelia Murray came from England to Mobile for a short stay. Later she wrote that in Mobile she found the Battle House to be "the best managed hotel I have met in the United States."

There were others, too, who stayed in the Battle House and liked it: Jefferson Davis and General Beauregard, Henry Clay and General Grant, Millard Fillmore and Admiral Semmes. Belle Boyd, the Confederate spy, was staying there when she was notified of the death of her boss, Stonewall Jackson. The list could go on and on.

The Battle House was a center of local social activity as well. The Grand Ballroom had been the scene of the major Mardi Gras balls since Reconstruction days. And the rich planters from the Black Belt left their plantations after the crops were laid away and flocked to Mobile. Almost every fashionable wedding in upper Alabama was followed by a honeymoon to Mobile where the young couples spent their most treasured hours together dancing in the Battle House ballroom and dining by candlelight.

One of the last of the world renowned visitors had come to the Battle House in 1898 on his way to Cuba to lead the Rough Riders in that gallant charge up San Juan Hill. Now, in 1905, he was back. This time, as President of the United States. Teddy made a speech in Bienville Square at the invitation of the Masons, then went around the corner to gaze upon the rubble of the Battle House Hotel. If the President thought that the Battle House was finished, he was dead wrong. Even as he stood there, forces were at work which would erect a bigger and better Battle House. The next year, some of Mobile's leading citizens formed a company, with D. R. Burgess as president, to begin construction and in 1908, the Battle House was open for business again.

Teddy Roosevelt ran for President in the election of 1912. But much as Mobilians admired Teddy, they were glad he was beaten. The Democrats were back in power after years of being on the outside and the man who had led them back into office was a native Southerner— Woodrow Wilson of Virginia!

Mobilians were elated. The Governor of Alabama immediately fired off an invitation to the President to address the Southern Commercial Congress to be held in Mobile. President Wilson quickly responded. He would come to Mobile if the crisis with Mexico did not flare up too seriously.

The news electrified the city. The new President had been somewhat of a mysterious figure to most of the nation. Scholarly and retiring, he had burst upon the national scene as somewhat of a nonentity. During the campaign, the spotlight had been on the colorful and energetic Bull Moose, Teddy Roosevelt. Even after his victory, Wilson had remained in relative seclusion. He had made no significant speeches, no spectacular public appearances. Now for the first time, he was coming out of his shell and he was coming to Mobile.

Early on the morning of October 27, 1913, the President stepped off the train and was led to a hastily built wooden platform. On his train ride through the heart of the South, he had been wildly greeted by throngs of admirers. With no less enthusiasm, the people of Mobile received him into their city. Mayor Pat Lyons made a short speech. Then a few other high officials put their two cents worth in the pot. "Woodrow Wilson," they said, "is a Southerner of giant intellectual attainments, as a famous educator and as a scholarly statesman."

After being called everything from a scholar to a prophet, the President remarked that he was hungry. The big-wigs got the point and the presidential party was led down Royal Street to the Battle House just in time for a good old-fashioned Southern breakfast. Wilson appeared to be the hungriest man at the table or, at least, he was the first to dig in. He reached for the grapefruit with one hand and stirred his hominy grits with the other. Then he began noisily chewing a piece of bacon. Bystanders were eyeing him closely to see how a President did it, but they found that he smacked about as much as anybody else.

When the illustrious guest had gobbled down a healthy dose of corn pones and broiled squab on toast, he leaned back and tried to digest his morning take. The Battle House provided violin music for this part of the program. Despite the wailing of strings, the breakfast must have settled well with the President for he soon arose from the table and announced that he was ready to begin the show.

The show began when the President walked out of the Battle House and stepped into a shining new convertible. It was a long, black, distinguished-looking automobile and the President hopped up on the back seat with Mrs. Wilson beside him. Then the band struck up a tune and the parade moved out.

Mobile had gone all out for the occasion. For months, the reception committees had been organized and were hard at work. A city-wide holiday had been declared, the schools were turned out and the port city was filled with visitors from New Orleans, Texas and Latin America. As the parade moved out Government Street, tens of thousands lined the streets, waving their flags and tall, silk hats. The procession took on the aura of a Roman triumphal march. Wilson was Caesar and Mobile was a conquered province.

By the time the parade had reached the Lyric Theater on Conti Street, there was evidence enough that Wilson had, indeed, conquered Mobile. Tons of confetti covered the streets and thousands of Mobilians surrounded the Lyric Theater. Only a few hundred could get in, though. And they were a select few, governors, congressmen, members of the press, city officials and secret service men all rose to attention as Woodrow Wilson mounted the speakers' platform.

Despite their elation at the President's visit, many officials had been dumbfounded when the President announced he would come to Mobile. During his first six months in office, he had received invitations from all of America's great cities. Why had he chosen Mobile to make his first significant public address? Perhaps now the mystery would be cleared up.

As the President moved into the heart of his speech, it became evident that he meant to direct his thoughts toward Latin America. He had recently embarked America on a new trend in foreign policy by refusing to recognize Mexico's new regime. "The Mexican revolutionaries are immoral," he said, "and the United States is under no obligation to recognize immoral governments." All well and good, but the truth was that Wilson had irked all Latin America by his actions. They accused him of trying to interfere in the internal affairs of a Latin American country. This bit of high handed action, coupled with Uncle Sam's long history of brusqueness in its Latin American dealings, had brought the country to a point of strained relations with its southern neighbors. Now Wilson would seek to make amends.

"The future is going to be very different for this hemisphere from the past," he said. "Interest does not tie nations together but sympathy and understanding do unite them, and I believe that the new Panama Canal that is about to be opened will spiritually unite the two continents. It is a spiritual union which we seek. . . ." The President's words were broken off by a round of applause, especially by the Latin American dignitaries.

Wilson then went into a discourse deliberately designed to allay the fears of nations of both hemispheres. In a single string of words he pronounced the death sentence to the great issue of American politics.

"The United States," he said, "will never again seek one added foot of territory by conquest."

Imperialism was dead and Wilson had buried it in

Mobile. His speech ended, the President received a tumultuous ovation, then was led back to the train station. Just as the train was pulling out, a city official hopped on board and presented the President with a medal which had been prepared for him as a memento. In the hectic five hours that Wilson had been in Mobile, the medal was the only thing forgotten.

The President's visit had added another exciting chapter to the Battle House's history. Some years later, the switchboard girl in the main lobby received a mysterious phone call from Daphne across the bay. "There's a very sick man upstairs in Room 552," the voice said. "You'd better go get a doctor."

"Who is this?" the operator asked. But all she heard was the click of a receiver. Alarmed, the operator notified the house detective who called Dr. S. H. Stephens. Together, the two men climbed to the fifth floor and walked into Room 552. The bedroom was slightly rumpled as though a scuffle had occurred. At the bathroom door, the two men stopped short. Lying on the floor in a pool of blood was Henry Butler, a young "bon vivant," son of a prominent Mobile realtor. He had been beaten and strangled to death.

It was the next day before the mystery began to unravel. Tracing the phone call to Daphne, police found two brothers missing from the community of Fairhope. The Dyson brothers, sons of a prominent Fairhope resident, were nowhere to be found. Police arrested the father and set up a nation-wide alert. Three days later, the brothers turned up in Jacksonville, Florida, where they were arrested and sent back to Mobile to be charged with murder.

For two months, Mobilians whispered about a possible motive while the Dyson brothers sat calmly in jail awaiting trial. "It was an affair of honor," is all they would say. To prove it, they hired B. F. McMillan and a young attorney who was to make quite a name for himself in later years, the eloquent Sam Johnston.

When court convened in November, Sam Johnston pleaded the younger Dyson not guilty by reason of insanity. The District Attorney asked for death in the electric chair. Dyson never denied the killing, but still maintained that it was an affair of honor. While the court was wondering what sort of honor was involved, Mrs. Dyson took the stand and confessed of intimacies with the departed Mr. Butler. She had met Butler at Fairhope several years before, she related, and an affair resulted that extended to Mobile and New Orleans. She had repented, she said, and had confessed everything to her husband, an act which had driven him to the verge of insanity and resulted in Butler's death.

Dyson, himself, was then called to testify but not before his sorrowful wife dramatically kissed him on the witness stand. All this and Johnston's description of the two little children waiting at home for their beloved parents was too much for the jury. They brought in a verdict of not guilty and Dyson walked out of the court room a free man. Several weeks later, Dyson's brother was also acquitted and the last thread of the Battle House murder was unraveled.

Chapter 17

Bart Chamberlain Fights the Felons

The man who had prosecuted the Dyson brothers was a native Mobilian, descendant of a family long prominent in legal circles. When Bart Chamberlain graduated from the University of Alabama Law School, he came back to Mobile and was elected to the State Legislature. After several years in Montgomery, he was elevated to the office of District Attorney, or State Solicitor, as it was then known, where he spent the rest of his life.

Over the next several decades, Bart Chamberlain was in the thick of every important event in Mobile's history until his death in 1943. He had seen the last yellow fever epidemic in 1897 and had heard William Jennings Bryan make his "free silver" speech at the old Lyric Theatre. He had seen the great hurricanes of 1893 and 1906. And now in 1916, he watched Mobile shudder in the face of another violent hurricane.

The tropical monster had burst upon Mobile at 5:00

A.M. on the morning of July 5th. By mid-morning the winds had reached a velocity of 105 miles per hour. Late in the afternoon, the storm veered to the southwest, pushing the water out of the bay and into the heart of the city. Royal Street was covered by two feet of salt water and then the flood moved across the city until it covered the whole business district.

Hundreds of citizens were trapped and had to spend the night downtown. Some went to hotels and some very prominent Mobilians spent their first night in jail as guests of the sheriff. The courthouse tower was destroyed, the clock faces were blown off and the rains flooded the courtrooms. The roof of the Cawthon Hotel was ripped off and a horse was electrocuted on Conception Street by a live wire. Old St. Matthew's Church was demolished and every house on the bay front from Shell Road to Bay Avenue was leveled. The bay boat *Carney* sank at the foot of Dauphin Street and the *Pleasure Bay* went to the bottom of One Mile Creek. Out from Monroe Park, the crew of the mailboat *Uncle Sam* leaped from her sides and swam ashore just as she was going to the bottom of the bay.

Newspapers across the land carried the bold headlines, "Twenty-two lives lost in Mobile," and "Mobile is wiped off the map." But it was not quite that bad. Mobile survived the hurricane but three years later in the backyard of Howard Cunningham's meat market, on Hamilton Street, a fire broke out. It was 3:25 P.M., May 21, 1919, when the fire department was notified. The trucks and wagons raced to the scene and quickly spread their hoses. But when the water was turned on little more than a trickle drizzled out the nozzle. The water pressure was so low that most of the fire-fighting had to be done by carrying buckets of water from the river, from private wells and homes.

Such measly efforts were no match for the big blaze once it got started. Leaping across Conception Street, the fire began to move toward the southeast with alarming velocity. Picking up steam, it spread to Royal and Canal Streets, then made its way to the Alabama Dry Dock and Shipbuilding Company. At this point several thousand volunteers made a last-ditch effort. They soaked the buildings and dynamited several nearby structures until the fire turned further southward and continued its destructive march.

After several more hours, the wind began to die down. By the time the sun had fallen for the day, the big fire had burnt itself out. But not before thousands of Mobilians had been left homeless and forty city blocks were ravaged. Surveying the damage the next day, Bart Chamberlain saw a ghastly forest of gaunt chimneys rising out of the ashes, an awful catastrophe for his first year in office. But the fire was only the crowning blow to a terrible year in Mobile's history. A few months before, on February 19, an explosion in a boiler factory had resulted in more death and destruction. Besides that, it had scared the daylights out of the whole city by the resulting power failure. During that same winter, Mobile had experienced the worst flu epidemic in its history, a disease so prevalent it laid the whole town low.

But Mobile came back. Survival was an old habit by now and Bart Chamberlain helped usher in a new era of prosperity and sensationalism. Bart the Barrister was made for his position. Courtly, suave and distinguished, Chamberlain was the prototype of the "Southern Gentleman." He was efficient, honorable and above all conscientious in the administration of justice. One example would serve to demonstrate: a popular policeman named Murphy was murdered at the corner of Broad and Conti. Several weeks later, a likely suspect named Clyde Beach was apprehended and Chamberlain prosecuted the case. The evidence appeared to be fairly conclusive and the jury wasted little time in bringing a sentence of life imprisonment. But for Bart Chamberlain, even a shred of doubt was an albatross around his neck. For years, the conscientious solicitor visited Beach at Kilby State Prison in hopes that the prisoner would confess. The conviction was less important to him than the satisfaction that justice had been done.

During his first ten years in office, Bart Chamberlain rang up a string of convictions that has hardly been equalled in the annals of Alabama jurisprudence. Then, in 1929, he ran into a young lawyer named Harry Seale. The irrepressible Harry presented an impressive figure. Long and lean, he seemed at one instance a prophet straight out of the Old Testament and on another, a character out of Charles Dickens.

In his younger days, Harry Seale had a peculiar habit of grunting in court. Most of the judges stoically tolerated Harry's antics, but Judge Tisdale J. Touart was a hard man to amuse. Harry snorted once too often one day and the sober Judge stopped court and proceeded to give Harry a lecture on the impropriety of grunting in court. When the judge had finished his lecture, Harry nodded and the trial was resumed. The opposing attorney made a statement, Harry objected, Judge Touart overruled the objection and Harry grunted.

"You have grunted for the last time in my courtroom," the judge said, disdainfully. "I hereby fine you five dollars."

Harry walked up to the bench, pulled out his wallet and slammed down a five dollar bill.

"That is no way to pay off a judge," said Touart. "That'll be five dollars more." Then Harry walked up to the bench, took out his wallet again and this time very gently laid down another five dollar bill. The judge fumed.

"I hereby fine you ten dollars," bellowed Judge Touart. "I find you in contempt of court and sentence you to six hours in jail." Then the judge called for the sheriff and Harry was carted away to jail, the first attorney in Alabama history to actually go to jail on a contempt charge. A few hours later, Harry hired an attorney, appealed the contempt charges and was out on bail.

It was not the first time Harry Seale had been held in contempt of court nor was it the last. Over the years, he had a running battle with a number of judges but always managed to retain a healthy respect for the law and a good disposition toward everybody. He had another habit of calling everybody "Colonel" and usually people would respond by calling him "Colonel," too. Once he called the Governor of Alabama "Colonel" and George Wallace responded by making Harry an honorary Colonel on the Governor's staff.

Over the years Harry Seale faced Bart Chamberlain in hundreds of cases and was a thorn in the District Attorney's side. Perhaps the most spectacular was the case of Elijah Henry Taylor.

It was on the afternoon of August 30, 1929, that Bart Chamberlain and Harry Seale first learned of the action that would bring them together in court. Just after noon, a lithe, hefty Negro walked into a machine shop in the southeast section of Mobile and sharpened his long knife on the grindstone. His brow was dripping with sweat as he moved out of the machine shop and down the street to the home of his wife's mother. His mother-in-law came to the door and said that her daughter Adele was not at home. But even as the words fell from her lips, the pregnant form of Adele Taylor appeared in the doorway.

"Get away from here, Henry," she screamed. "I don't want nothing to do with you ever no more."

Elijah looked blankly at his young wife. She was eight months with child and bulging. But he didn't think of that. He thought of the six times she had hauled him into court and how the court had seized his wages and left him penniless. And now he had no job but she had gone back to the judge, asking for more money. Elijah's eyes flashed. The sweat streamed from his forehead as he leaped up the steps and knocked his mother-in-law down. Bounding into the room, he looked for his wife but she hid behind the curtain, then ran out the door and down the street. Her sister attacked Elijah and he slashed her with the big knife. Then Elijah ran out the door and down the street in a mad rush for his fleeing wife.

Followed by a screaming mother and a bleeding sister, the pregnant woman ran for her life down the hot pavement. At the corner of Hamilton and Madison Streets, the fleeing woman, exhausted and out of breath, stumbled and fell, face-down. She had crawled but a few feet when Elijah, like a big cat, pounced upon her and straddled her prostrate body. With his left hand he grabbed her by the hair and pulled her head back as far as it would go, then took his knife and slit her throat, almost severing her head.

The two in-laws rushed up, then fell on the ground in abject horror. Elijah sat down by the side of his wife and watched her bleed to death. Calmly, he pulled out a pouch of tobacco and began rolling himself a cigarette. An officer named Joe Chaillot happened along at this point and tried to extract a confession from the killer.

"Want me to roll it for you?" asked the officer. "You got too much blood on your hands."

"I don't give a damn," snapped Elijah. "The more blood, the better I like it."

Elijah was carted away to jail and his dying wife was rushed to the hospital where a hasty Caesarean failed to save the life of the baby.

When the case reached Circuit Court in November, Bart Chamberlain dwelt on the incontrovertible facts of the killing, the admission of guilt and the cold-bloodedness of the act. Harry Seale brought scores of Taylor's family to the stand, as well as people who had been close to him during his formative years. Before he was through, Seale had proved that nearly everybody in Taylor's family was insane; but there was still some question about Elijah, himself.

On the ninth of November, 1929, the accused man stood before Judge Joel Goldsby after the jury brought forth a verdict of guilty. "The Warden of Kilby State Prison," read the Judge, "shall cause to pass through your body, Elijah Henry Taylor, a current of electricity of sufficient intensity to cause your death." Judge Goldsby's voice resounded through the hushed chamber as all ears in the crowded courtroom strained to catch the words of the sentence. Here and there a woman's sob contrasted strangely with the judge's strong voice. During the pause, the prisoner's head bowed, his face paled and he slumped forward in faint. But Judge Goldsby did not notice. "And the applied continuance of such current through your body, Elijah Henry Taylor, until you, Elijah Henry Taylor, are dead."

With sentence passed, the trial was over. The condemned man was taken to his cell to await execution, Bart Chamberlain congratulated himself on another conviction and Harry Seale went back to his law office. Later on that evening, Harry was visited by a mysterious stranger who said his name was John F. Kelly. Harry recognized the name but it belonged to a different face than the John F. Kelly he had selected for jury duty. The John F. Kelly standing before him had been out of town when the jury summons was mailed to him and knew nothing about the trial until he read in the newspaper that he had been one of the jurors that convicted Elijah Henry Taylor. A quick check by Seale revealed that the other John F. Kelly had been told by a friend that his name was on the jury list published in the newspaper. He had gone to the courtroom, was accepted as a juror and knew nothing about the other John F. Kelly.

With this development, Harry Seale appealed the case of Elijah Henry Taylor to the Alabama Supreme Court. After some deliberation that high court declared a mistrial and on May 4, 1931, the case was begun all over again. Bart Chamberlain was furious but nevertheless prosecuted the case as vigorously as before, again asking the death penalty for Taylor. This time, however, Harry Seale was more successful. On May 6, Elijah Henry Taylor was sentenced to life imprisonment. In jail, Taylor proved himself to be a model prisoner, eventually was released from prison, landed a good job, and lived happily ever after.

It was a bitter defeat for Bart Chamberlain but he had little use for tears. It would soon be time for another round in the courtroom with Harry Seale and with Sam Johnston.

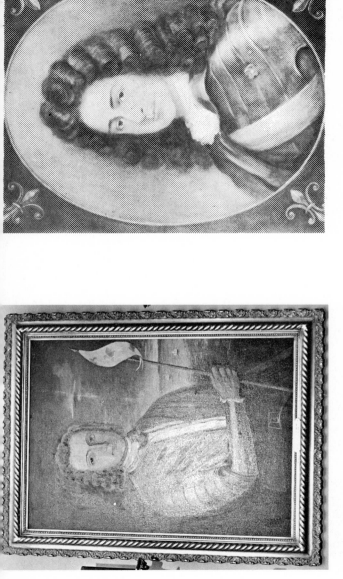

Pierre Le Moyne, Sieur d'Iberville
(1661–1706)

Jean-Baptiste Le Moyne, Sieur de Bienville
(1680-1767)

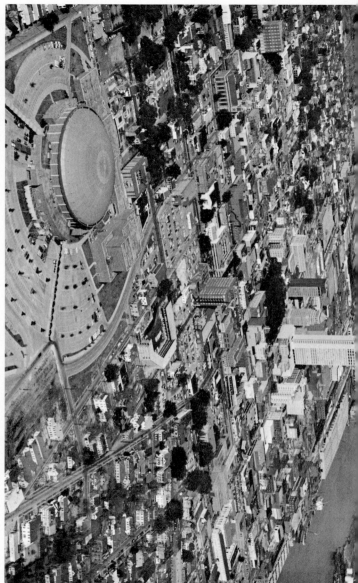

Photo by John Spottswood

The city of Mobile, Alabama projects a striking image of progress, pride, and tradition. One of the nation's ten largest seaports, it is the home of the Senior Bowl, Junior Miss Pageant, Azalea Trail, Alabama Deep Sea Fishing Rodeo, Alabama's tallest skyscraper, Mardi Gras and many more world famous attractions.

Henri de Tonty
"The Iron Hand"

Photo by Frank Brown   Courtesy Phoenix Museum

Addin Lewis
Mobile's First Mayor

Photo by Frank Brown   Courtesy Phoenix Museum

Lafayette strikes an elegant pose in this painting made at the time of his visit to Mobile.

Mobile's First Board of Commissioners - 1911

at J. Lyons   Laz Schwarz   Harry Pillans

his photo of the staff, taken in front of the second home of
ie First National Bank, was made in 1875 on St. Francis Street.

Courtesy Mobile Press Register
Madame Octavia Walton
Le Vert

Courtesy Mobile Press Register
Augusta Evans Wilson

Courtesy Mobile Press Register
John Forsyth

Courtesy Mobile Press Register
Captain Peter Alba

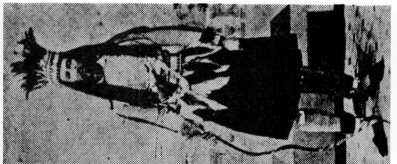

Courtesy Mobile Press Register
Joseph Stillworth Cain
"Chief Slacabamorinico"

Courtesy Mobile Press Register
Admiral
Raphael Semmes

Courtesy Mobile Press Register

Father Michael Portier

Courtesy Mobile Press Register

Father Abraham Joseph Ryan

"The Charm Spot of the Deep South," as Bellingrath Gardens and Home is referred to, attracts worldwide attention with its beauty and floral perfection.

Walter D. Bellingrath

A common sight during the early 1900's, street cars drawn by horses carted Mobilians to their various destinations in high style.

John Fowler had the responsibility of keeping the clock at the City Hall working well, when he was not tinkering with "flying machines."

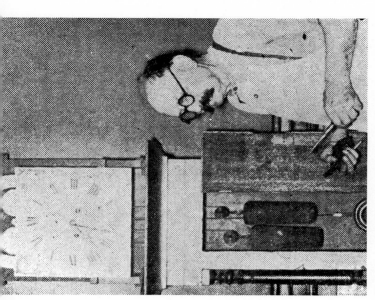

Bishop Wilmer

Courtesy Mobile Press Register

John Fowler, watchmaker, constructed this "airplane" in Monroe Park before the famous Wright Brothers flight at Kittyhawk, North Carolina.

Photo by Frank Brown   *Courtesy First National Bank*

This painting of the "Nettie Quill," one of the many riverboats which traveled the Mobile area rivers, hangs in the First National Bank Building.

Photo by Frank Brown   *Courtesy First National Bank*

The "John Quill," shown at the loading docks, depicts the era of "King Cotton" on the Mobile waterfront.

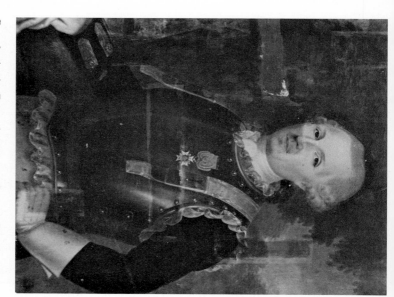

Antoine Phillipe de Marigny de Mandeville
Commander of Fort Condé

General James Wilkinson

General Andrew Jackson

General Braxton Bragg

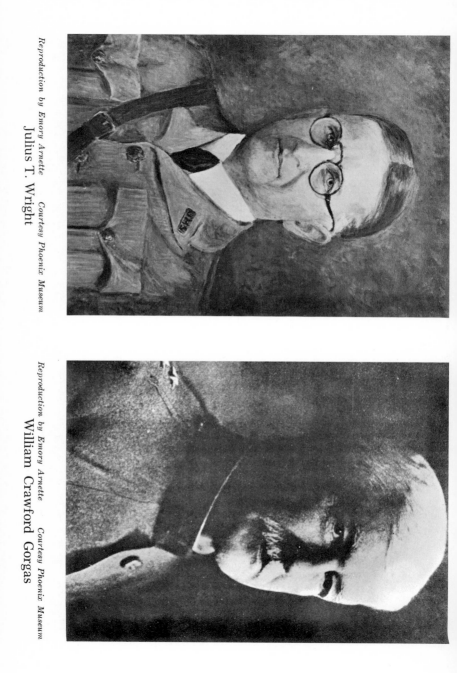

Hatchett Chandler, after much legal controversy, was finally interred at his beloved Fort Morgan on the Gulf of Mexico to remain eternally amidst the relics of his fondest memories and most exciting Civil War tales.

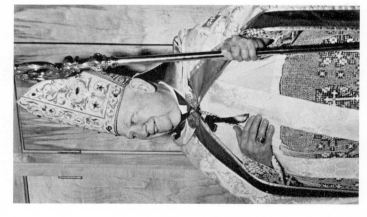

Bishop Toolen, head of the Mobile diocese for many years, is a dedicated citizen and promoter of Mobile as well as a faithful servant of the Catholic Church.

The Stephen Croom Home, located on the corner of Charles and Augusta Streets, has been continually occupied by the Croom family for 125 years.

Twelve Oaks, facing Washington Square at Chatham and Palmetto Streets, depicts its era with charm and grace.

This white-columned ante bellum mansion is the Mitchell Home (originally the Bragg Home), located on Springhill Avenue.

Oakleigh, Mobile's official ante bellum mansion and headquarters of the Historic Mobile Preservation Society, was constructed entirely by slave labor under the direction of James W. Roper.

If one looks closely the brick pavement on St. Joseph Street is visible along with the watering trough and carriage of 1909.

The tiered fountain in Bienville Square lends a touch of old South charm to downtown Mobile.

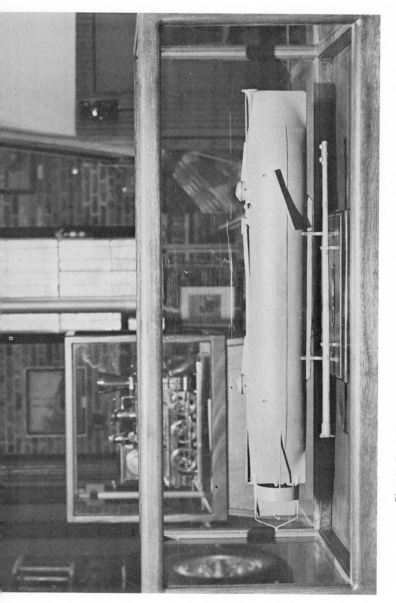

Photo by Frank Brown

Courtesy Phoenix Museum

This model of the "Hunley," which was the first submarine built in Mobile, is preserved at the Phoenix Firehouse Museum.

Courtesy First National Bank

Looking east on Royal Street a 1908 Mobilian's view would resemble this photo. The old Customs House (flying flag) three story First National Bank Building.

Courtesy First National Bank

The corner of Royal and St. Francis during Mardi Gras 1904, with the "old" Battle House on the right offers a glimpse of long skirts, street cars and horse-drawn carriages.

Courtesy First National Bank

February 13, 1905—the ashes of Mobile's
famous old Battle House Hotel serve as a tragic
frame for this shot of the Customs House.

Courtesy First National Bank

Bienville Square, in the heart of Mobile, is clearly visible
in this 1908 shot, along with the "new" Sheraton Battle
House on the left and the masts of sailing ships at the docks.

The Bankhead Tunnel under Mobile Bay, shown here during construction, has greatly decreased time and distance reaching the eastern shore.

This aerial view of Mobile near her waterfront shows Alabama State Dry Docks, one of the top ten ports in the nation.

Frank Boykin

Bishop William Thomas Phillips, Th.B., D.D., LL.D. Founder and Organizer of the A.O.H., Church of God, Inc.

The International Paper Company Mill Complex, one of the largest paper manufacturers and converters in the world, also promotes good will and progress in the Mobile area.

Courtesy of International Paper Company

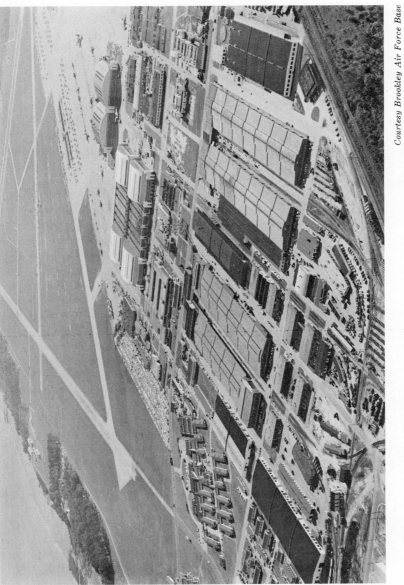

Gigantic Brookley Field, one of the nation's ten largest, most efficient Air Force Bases and supply depots brought employment and industry to Mobile.

Mobilians were proud of their first piece of automotive fire fighting equipment shown here on St. Joseph Street in the early 1900's.

Crowds of Mobilians turned out when Teddy Roosevelt participated in the dedication of the new Masonic Lodge.

Photo by Frank Brown   Courtesy Mobile Jaycees

Mobile Azalea Trail Maids, Pat Register and Sandra Henderson receive the autograph of former Governor George C. Wallace on their trip to Montgomery.

Photo by Frank Brown   Courtesy Mobile Jaycees

Jack Edwards, First District United States Congressman of which Mobile is a part, speaks at the Jaycees' Fourth of July Celebration.

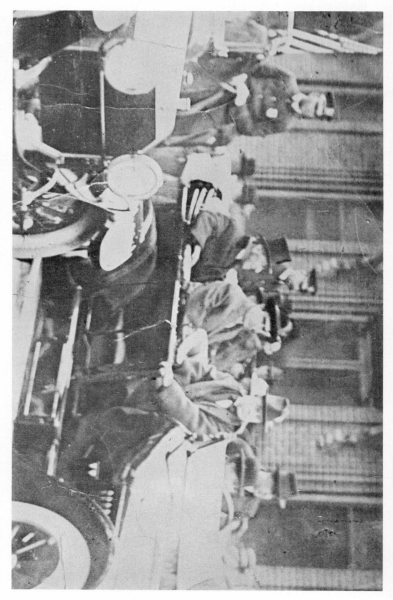

During his visit to the "Port City" in 1914, President Woodrow Wilson was presented to the citizens of Mobile in a motorcade and honored with a breakfast.

Courtesy of Mr. Henry Franetich

George A. Haas

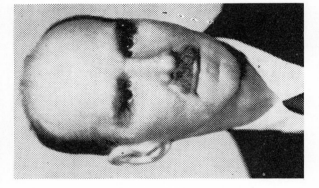

E. Herndon Smith

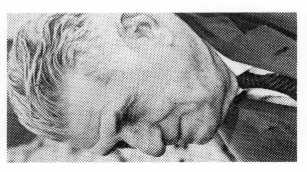

Peter Hamilton

Photo by Frank Brown

Early French, Spanish and American settlers, many victims of yellow fever and cholera, are buried in raised tombs in the old Church Street Cemetery began in 1819.

Photo by Frank Brown

One of numerous familiar graves is that of Joe Cain, Chief Slacabamorinico, who reinstated the Mardi Gras Carnival after the Civil War.

Photo Frank Brown Courtesy Mobile Jaycees

The Quigley Home now houses the offices of Mobile's Junior Chamber of Commerce, sponsors of the Azalea Trail, Junior Miss Pageant, Alabama Deep Sea Fishing Rodeo and many more civic projects.

Photo Frank Brown Courtesy Mobile Jaycees

The previous home of the Mobile Junior Chamber of Commerce was much smaller but served Mobile and her tourists just as efficiently as her present, more lavish office in the Quigley Home.

Debi Faubion (seated), America's Junior Miss for 1968, is surrounded by (left to right) Christine Barker, New Mexico, 3rd Runner-up; Julie Stonecipher, Washington, 1st Runner-up, Brenda Wood, Oregon, 2nd Runner-up and Donna Linderman, New York, 4th Runner-up.

Azalea Trail Maids welcome Lorne Greene, of
"Bonanza" fame, to Mobile. Greene was Master of Ceremonies at the 1968 America's Junior Miss Pageant.

The arrival of the Junior Misses in Mobile is a festive affair with
a special greeting from the Azalea Trail Maids and the Jaycees.

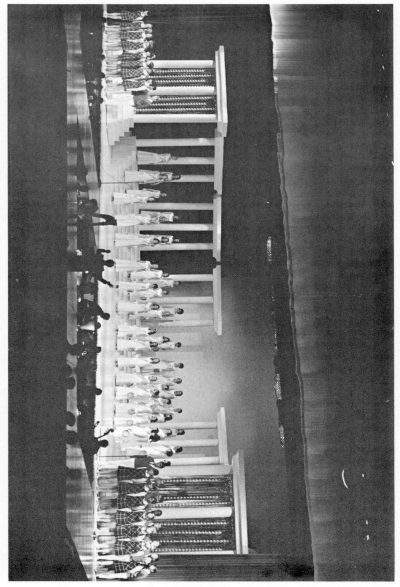

America's Junior Miss Pageant held at Mobile's Municipal Auditorium includes fifty of the nation's loveliest high school senior girls to compete in fields of talent, appearance, poise and intelligence.

Photo by Frank Brown   *Courtesy Mobile Jaycees*

One of the Jaycee projects, the Alabama Deep
Sea Fishing Rodeo, offers adventure, fun and
reward for fishermen from across the nation.

Photo by Frank Brown   *Courtesy Mobile Jaycees*

The fish do come big and plentiful at
the Alabama Deep Sea Fishing Rodeo.

The glitter and excitement of Mardi Gras Carnival parades attract visitors from around the world to share in the prizes and laughter with native Mobilians.

These Mobile Belles, Azalea Trail Maids, reflect the city's charm, elegance and hospitality.

The annual Soap Box Derby is just one of numerous activities promoting the interest of Mobile's younger set.

Courtesy Mobile Press Register

This statue of Bernardo De Galvez stands in the new Spanish Plaza completed recently in cooperation with Mobile's sister city of Malaga, Spain.

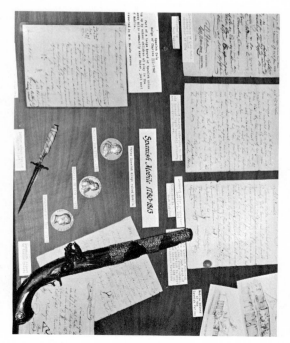

Photo by Frank Brown

Courtesy Phoenix Museum

Relics and documents of the Spanish era in Mobile (1780-1813) lie encased for visitors at the Phoenix Museum.

Courtesy University of South Alabama

This recent aerial view of the University of South Alabama campus depicts some of the vibrant construction growth the Mobile-centered school has realized over the past four years of its existence.

This beautiful South American Jaguar, unnamed as yet, has become the University of South Alabama's newest mascot.

The University of South Alabama's new four story $2.5 million library will ultimately house 125,000 volumes and will have a total capacity to hold 330,000 volumes.

Photo by Frank Brown

Courtesy Spring Hill College

This view down the "Avenue of the Oaks" to the President's home at Spring Hill College depicts the charm and grace of Alabama's oldest institution of higher learning.

St. Joseph's Cathedral on the Spring Hill College campus signifies the constructive impressiveness of the historic institution.

The new Campus Center for Spring Hill students strikes a dramatic but modern contrast to the cathedral.

Photo by Frank Brown

Now on exhibit on Mobile Bay causeway, the USS Alabama is shown here passing through the Panama Canal on her journey home to be restored.

Photo by Frank Brown

Halftime at the Senior Bowl Football Game at Ladd Memorial Stadium is a colorful extravaganza of majorettes, ante bellum belles and marching bands.

The Greater Gulf State Fair, through the help of
the Mobile Jaycees, draws thousands of exhibits
and people to Hartwell Field each October.

Barton Academy, Mobile's oldest public school, now houses the offices of Mobile School Board.

Chapter 18

Billy Sunday and Demon Rum

The great Billy Sunday stormed into Mobile on New Year's Day to open the fabulous year of 1927. The fire-breathing evangelist had been giving 'em hell from coast to coast ever since the Volstead Act had opened up the roaring twenties. Now it was Mobile's turn to catch a little hell and Billy really socked it to 'em. He opened up his campaign by preaching three times in the tabernacle at St. Anthony and Royal Streets and for each sermon the tabernacle was filled to the brim. Appropriately enough, Billy's initial sermon was devoted to the wages of sin and the particular villain was demon rum.

"There are men among you today," he thundered, "that when they die, they won't need to have a sermon preached. Just put a bottle of whiskey on their coffin and that will tell the story of their lives."

Night and day for six long weeks, the fiery evangelist fulminated against the booze hounds and the boot-

leggers. He might start out on various topics but he
would always get back to the whiskey sermon which he
would conclude with his favorite slogan:

"We don't need more booze,
We need more Bible.
We don't need more jag,
We need more Jesus.
We don't need more grub,
We need more God."

During the campaign, almost everybody in Mobile
made at least one trip to the revival. The first night out,
Billy asked everyone to stand and make a New Year's
resolution never to break the Ten Commandments again.
There were those who tried but their style was severely
cramped. Some didn't even try because they smelled
something brewing and it wasn't tea. In truth, the congregation couldn't help smelling the brew because it
came at them from every direction. There were stills on
Mon Louis Island, out in the Mobile Delta, at Magazine
Point and right in the heart of the city. Nevertheless,
Billy kept preaching and the people kept repenting.
When he left after six weeks, Billy pronounced the revival a glorious success and he thanked all the people in
Mobile for their cooperation and support. Especially did
he thank the *Mobile Register* for the front page publicity
devoted to his services. Every day during the course of
the revival there had been an article on his sermons and
every day the article had been almost completely surrounded by articles on rum-running, still raids and liquor
conspiracies.

It was only natural that Billy Sunday had concen-
trated so hard on Mobile. All during the twenties the
liquor flowed into the port city more swiftly than almost
any other city in the nation. Mobile was ideal as a port of

entry for the big smugglers. Quiet and unsuspecting, the city was always understaffed in law enforcement personnel. Mobile had no need to waste money on a plethora of policemen.

When the Volstead Act had first amended the Constitution, few liquor dealers took it seriously. Flagrant violations were the order of the day. After several years, the Federal Government decided to clamp down hard on the violators. The Volstead Act Enforcement Crusade swung into operation and its first big target was Mobile, Alabama. Izzy Einstein, the renowned Federal prohibition agent, came to Mobile and found the county saturated with liquor coming from Cuba and sold as openly as orange juice. Then came the Federal District Attorney, Aubrey Broyles, who was to upset the applecart. Mobile was, according to Broyles, designed by authorities in Washington to be the example of the most thoroughly cleansed city in America and the program of the Enforcement Crusade would base its policies on results obtained in Mobile.

Accordingly, the Federal agents swooped down on Mobile in November of 1923. They seized a hundred thousand dollars worth of booze in the first few days and uncovered what they claimed to be a giant rum ring. The Federal grand jury opened hearings in November and heard testimony until Christmas Eve. When it finished its work in December, the results were shocking. The grand jury called for indictments against 117 leading men of the community. They were promptly arrested and the first trials set for May, 1924.

In the May trials, the prosecution directed their attacks at the local dealers on charges of violating the Prohibition Act. They had to get the front men before they could get the men behind the scenes. After a trying week, the Government succeeded in convicting six men. Geronimo Perez, Dan Jemison, James F. Daves and three others were sent off to the Federal pen in Atlanta to cool off for awhile. They didn't cool off much, though. The longer they sat in the cooler, the warmer they became and by the time the big trial rolled around in February 1925, their cells were boiling. The Federal men told the convicts they could get a bit of fresh air by agreeing to testify in Mobile. Fresh air sounded pretty good to the ex-liquor dealers. By this time, they were afflicted as much by claustrophobia as they were by homesickness. So back to Mobile came the home town boys to testify against their former rummates.

When the great trials began in February, Mobilians were aghast to find among the accused the names of their Sheriff, Paul Cazalas, their Legislator and ex-sheriff, William H. Holcombe and their Chief of Police, Patrick J. O'Shaughnessy. Added to this were such well known figures as Frank Boykin, George L. "Tricky" Donaghue, Captain Jewett Scott, Robert Holcombe, Judge J. B. Connaughton, W. J. Hanlon and "Mr. Mardi Gras" Alfred Staples. To represent them, the accused had hired the cream of the Mobile Bar Association, Francis Inge, Gregory L. Smith, and Sam Johnston.

As court convened all of the indicted took their seats except Frank Boykin. Out on bail, he came stumbling in the courtroom fifteen minutes late.

"Where have you been?" the Judge demanded. Boykin looked up on the bench and saw Judge W. I. Grubb scowling down at him.

"I went to the wrong courtroom," said Boykin, sheepishly. A howl of laughter broke among the crowded spectators. Judge Grubb banged his gavel, then gave them all a dirty look. After order was restored the special prosecutor from Birmingham, Hugo Black, walked to the front to open the case against the conspirators. Black, a recent Ku Klux Klan dropout, had lost interest in burning crosses; he had found it more interesting to burn people. By his heated prosecutions, it was soon obvious that he meant to burn the Mobilians. He was so vigorous, one might have imagined he was running for the Supreme Court or something. Black charged the accused with conspiring to smuggle liquor into the United States and called to the stand Dan Jemison, one of the ex-Mobilians who now had an Atlanta mailing address. Snorting mad, Jemison began to squeal while his right hand was still in the air. "There really was a rum ring," he confessed, "and I was a part of it." Then he went on to describe how the liquor was transferred off Cuban ships twelve miles out in the Gulf and smuggled up the Mobile River to a place in Saraland.

"How did you become involved in this ring?" Hugo Black asked him.

"Frank Boykin talked me into it," said Jemison. "He talked us all into it."

"Who is 'us all'?" asked Hugo Black with feigned innocence.

" 'Us all,' " said Jemison, "is all us sitting before this court." Then he looked over the field and pointed to a sheepish-looking crew composed of Alfred Staples, William Holcombe and "Tricky" Donaghue. "There they set," said Jemison and the accused began to squirm.

Then Jemison went on to tell how the split occurred between local and Federal law enforcement officers.

"It was late one night in May, 1923," said Jemison. "The night of the Sam Powe raid. I called the jail that night and told them some liquor had been seized by the

Federal men at Sam Powe's house. They seized a carload of liquor in the driveway after a woman ran from the car and mysteriously disappeared in the woods. But they wouldn't go into the house until they had obtained a search warrant. After I told them that, the sheriff and some of his deputies went down there to Sam Powe's house and went in before the warrant arrived and took all the liquor away from the Federal men."

"What did the sheriff do with all the liquor?" asked Hugo Black. Jemison hesitated and the courtroom rocked with laughter. Judge Grubb banged his gavel and the snickering subsided until Jemison spoke again.

"I guess you'll have to ask the sheriff about that," he said and the courtroom exploded once more.

As soon as the judge got things in order, the next witness for the United States appeared. James F. Daves, another one of the transfers from Atlanta, took the stand and told his version of how he came to take the rap. "I was supposed to handle the liquor after we got it off the ship," he said. "I was to get rid of it to Chicago or New Orleans and some other places."

"Well, did you?" asked Hugo.

"Yessir, I did," said Daves. "I got rid of a bunch of it." The courtroom began to rumble and Judge Grubb gave a mean look. Daves looked around at the spectators. He didn't think it was so funny, himself, so he continued.

"I was supposed to get protection," he said. "The big boys were supposed to see to that. But when the Federal men came, they took all my stock and I got sent to the brig. Not much protection to that."

Hugo Black, sensing that a dangerous ripple of laughter was about to break, stepped up quickly and posed another question. "You mean they left you holding the booze? They made no further effort to help you or even contact you?"

"I was contacted the other day when I came in from Atlanta," said Daves. "I was offered $17,000 not to testify."

"Why $17,000?" asked Black.

"That's the amount I lost in the raid," said Daves.

"Well, why didn't you take it?" asked Black.

"I was going to," said Daves. "I told them I would. I got in my car and was on my way to close the deal a few hours ago."

"Well, what happened?" asked Black, incredulously. All eyes of the court fell on the squirming James F. Daves. He bowed his head, twisted his collar and looked at his shoetops.

"I ran out of gas," he managed to say. Then pandemonium broke in the Mobile courtroom. A great howl rocked the rafters of the building, followed by a burst of applause. Above the din could barely be heard the rapping of Judge Grubb's gavel. The judge finally stood up and bellowed at the congregation.

"If there is any more laughing in this courtroom today," yelled the judge, "I will clear the house." Not wanting to miss a good show, the spectators settled down for awhile.

Hugo Black continued to call witness after witness before the court.

Ike Cohen, a produce dealer, took the stand and testified that he and Frank Boykin had thought up a grand scheme of shipping carloads of booze to Chicago, disguised as tar. And Howard Warren, a Mobile chemist, testified that Frank Boykin brought him a sample of the rum to test.

"What was your report?" prodded Hugo Black.

"I said 'it tastes pretty good to me'," replied Warren. The courtroom broke up again but by this time Judge Grubb had given up on the laughter prohibition. When the final witness for the prosecution had been called, Hugo Black sat down and gave the floor to a splendid array of defense attorneys. Gregory L. Smith moved for dismissal of charges but the motion was denied. Then Francis J. Inge and Sam Johnston began to parade half of Mobile past the witness stand to testify to the good character of the accused. All the witnesses were unanimous in the opinion that the accused would never think of doing such a thing as these foreigners were claiming. One witness told of the time that Sheriff Holcombe helped her grandmother across Royal Street. One told of the time Alfred Staples lent her five dollars without even expecting any interest and another told of Frank Boykin feeding fresh peanuts to the squirrels in Bienville Square. The parade lasted for several days and it got thicker and thicker. Just as the accused were approaching sainthood, the parade came to a halt and the defense counsel tried a new line. They would now bring to the stand the defendants themselves. The climactic hour had arrived.

As Frank Boykin came to the stand, the crowds were hushed in anticipation of a great revelation. But all Frank did was to deny every question Hugo Black put to him. He so earnestly denied any knowledge of the running of the rum that his closest friends began to wonder if he were aware that a prohibition law had been passed. The judge and the jury, however, appeared to be more skeptical. Then the rest of the defendants came before the court and likewise denied everything they could think of. When the denials were complete, a brief recess was held, while District Attorney Aubrey Broyles visited Circuit Court. While the Mobile boys were being tried in Federal Court, the Federal boys were being tried in the Mobile Court.

Meanwhile, Hugo Black was preparing to deliver his final blow of the axe, Police Chief O'Shaughnessy was resigning from his office and the local residents were organizing a citizens' league to protest the outcome of the trial, whatever way it came out. When the court re-convened, Hugo Black and the defense attorneys had their final say and the jury left the courtroom to try to untangle the maze of conflicting testimony. On the twenty-first of February, the jury returned after twenty-two hours of deliberation to disappoint the crowd. "Not guilty," they said. And the spectators' faces were long and drawn. They had come to see some action. They brightened up a bit when the judge announced that court would reconvene the following day and that the accused would be prosecuted on another charge, conspiring to bribe Federal prohibition agents. Hugo Black was determined to burn somebody, else he might have to go back to burning crosses.

Again the defense counsel denied everything while the prosecution brought a couple of unimpressive witnesses before the stand. Then Hugo Black made his big move. "I call to the stand," he announced in melodramatic overtones, "the United States District Attorney, the Honorable Aubrey Broyles."

The spectators turned and saw the dapper Mr. Broyles tripping up the aisle. He was a popular figure among some people of Mobile, particularly among the church-going teetotalers who saw him as a Sir Galahad going

forth, in the name of God, to slay the Demon called
Rum. His fans clapped and cheered and looked around
contemptuously at those who were hissing. They were
still clapping when Broyles took the oath and began to
tell a story so fantastic some people believed it.

"Frank Boykin came to my house early in May, 1923,"
he said, "and demanded to know why I hadn't stayed in
Washington when I got his telegram."

"What telegram?" asked Hugo Black.

"I don't know," said Broyles. "I never got any telegram. He told me he had a long talk with Jess Smith, a
close friend of Attorney General Harry Daughterty. The
Attorney General said that Andrew Mellon, Secretary of
Treasury, had loaned the Republican Party $5,000,000.
The party had only paid back $2,000,000 and didn't know
how they were going to get back the rest."

"Go on," said Black.

"Well," continued Broyles, "the plan according to Boykin was for the district attorneys to be in charge of collecting taxes on liquor. The more we let through, the
more taxes we could collect. And we only had to turn
over part of the bribe money to the Republican Party,
just enough to cover the two million dollar debt."

When Broyles had finished giving more details of the
operation, Hugo Black looked at him mischievously and
posed the big question. "Just what was your answer to all
this?" he asked.

"I told him I was not interested," said Broyles. "Then
I made notes and immediately reported the whole plan
to Washington."

The courtroom gave way to a disorder of murmuring
and the judge pounded on the bench for attention. The

Defense attorneys were arguing among themselves and shouting instructions across the room. Defense witnesses then testified that Broyles was lying, that originally he was a member of a group trying to make a killing, that he had got cold feet, wanted more money, then backed out. But for the shouting, it was all over. A Federal prohibition agent named M. T. Gonzualles took the stand and claimed the accused attempted to bribe him and apparently the jury believed him. This time, they returned to the courtroom and handed down sentences that rocked the port city. Frank Boykin and William H. Holcombe were given two year sentences which they immediately appealed. Alfred Staples and Robert Holcombe were granted a mistrial while Patrick J. O'Shaughnessy and "Tricky" Donaghue got off with two years. Judge Connaughton was acquitted but scores of Mobilians were heavily fined.

Hugo Black, as a result of all the publicity, won election to the United States Senate before being appointed to the Supreme Court. But if he were elected because of his successful prosecution of the liquor cases, the voters were a little bit premature. Two years later, the appeals of Boykin, Holcombe and the others reached the Supreme Court before Black got there and the highest court turned the whole business over to the Circuit Court of Appeals. "Insufficient evidence," they ruled and the show was back on the road. The show didn't last too much longer, though. A few years later, Roosevelt rolled into office, the Volstead Act was repealed and the era of Demon Rum was over.

Chapter 19

The Fabulous Willie Mae

Foster Hale sat in his St. Michael Street law office on the afternoon of June 16, 1931. Business was slow, as it had been the past several years. He leaned back in his chair, folded his hands behind his head and stared out the window. Things just hadn't gone right these past several years. The stock market crash had ruined him, had taken away all his investments in one fell swoop. His only source of income now would be his law practice. But in the heat of the depression clients were as scarce as cold, hard cash. He hadn't had a paying client in over two months. Though he didn't look it, he was feeling all of his fifty-four years.

Then, a knock at the door. Foster Hale wheeled around expectantly. Maybe this would be a cash-paying customer.

"Come in!" he almost yelled. Then he relaxed and tried to appear as though he were busy at his desk.

The door slowly opened and Foster Hale's eyes fell on the bare ankles of a woman moving slowly toward his

MOBILE

desk. He looked up quickly and his pulse froze. The scowling eyes of Willie Mae Clausen looked down at him with obvious dissatisfaction.

"Did you get my telegram?" she demanded. But Foster Hale was too shocked to immediately reply. He only stared at her hardened features. At 33, her face was beginning to show the wear and tear of a hectic life.

Once she had been beautiful. Foster Hale's thoughts went back to that day in 1910 when he first had laid eyes on Willie Mae. She was only thirteen then, when she came wandering into his law office and told him a pitiful story of how her life's greatest desire was to go to school, to be a school teacher, and to do some great service. But she would never be able to do it, she said, because her aged parents were unable to work and she had no money, whatsoever.

Then he had lent her some money, told her to study hard and to pay it back whenever she could. Willie Mae had taken the money, studied hard but when she came back the next year she had shown such an amazing development that Foster forgot about her paying back the money. Over the next few months a heated romance developed between the suave, thirty-five-year-old attorney and the fourteen-year-old child-woman, despite the fact that he was already married. Willie Mae fell wildly in love with her benefactor and he promised to get a divorce and marry her when she became sixteen.

Apparently, the love affair was in full swing when Willie Mae reached her sixteenth birthday. Then she suffered her life's first disillusionment. Foster still loved her, he assured Willie Mae, but his wife would not give him a divorce. Or so he told her. But Willie Mae had never believed that story. His career and his social prestige were the real reasons, she thought.

And so Willie Mae, crest fallen and heartsick, found herself another man and married him, out of sheer spite. His name was Jesse Pugh and he hardly knew what hit him. After the young beauty latched on to him and married him, she talked him into moving to Birmingham where she could forget her lost lover.

But Willie Mae Pugh could not forget Foster Hale. After a while she dragged the unfortunate Jesse Pugh back to Mobile and found her way back into the life of Foster Hale. The romance had a new birth and began to blossom all over again. Foster gave her some money; her husband discovered the money, then demanded to know where she got it. Willie Mae told him the whole story and Mr. Pugh was off and running. After the divorce, Willie Mae again pledged her love to Foster and wanted to know when he would marry her. "Why, as soon as the divorce comes through," he promised. In the meantime, he stationed her in a fancy apartment in Biloxi, bought her some clothes and a car and made periodic visits to see her.

After a few years, Willie Mae began to despair again. Deeply hurt, she found another husband named Fred Clausen and went away to try again. Still, she could not forget. She began to correspond with Foster and the attorney eagerly answered her letters. He still adored her, he said, but it was "fate that keeps us apart."

Then the long-suffering Mr. Clausen discovered the love letters. When questioned, Willie Mae admitted that she still loved Foster Hale and that admission cost her another husband. Back she came to Mobile in search of her benefactor. Again he was waiting with open arms. The attorney took her back in more lavish style than ever, rented an expensive apartment, gave her $65 dollars a week to throw around and pledged his undying love.

Then, one cool day in October, fate intervened. Foster Hale was only one of the thousands of investors ruined by the Wall Street crash. But more than anyone else in Mobile, his personal life was affected by the fiasco. For it drained him of the small fortune by which he was able to support a wife, a family and a mistress. Sadly, he broke the news to Willie Mae, promising to do the best he could by her and once more pledging his eternal love. Willie Mae appeared to understand and graciously accepted the verdict. She went away for awhile to live with some in-laws in Atmore.

But over the next few years as the depression began to get worse, that seed of suspicion that haunts the soul of womanhood began to take root in the mind of Willie Mae Clausen—there was another woman, a younger, more attractive woman and Foster Hale was not broke. He was using his money to support the new woman in his life.

Furiously, Willie Mae came back to Mobile and confronted Foster Hale with the idea. She fumed and fussed and cried, then completely broke down. Foster picked her up and took her home. Then, fearing for her sanity, he dipped into his last bit of cash and paid a psychiatrist to give her some lengthy treatments. Before the treatments were over, Hale had to mortgage his property and borrow to the hilt to complete payment. When the treatment was over, Hale was satisfied that Willie Mae was back to normal and he returned her to Atmore.

Willie Mae was far from cured, however, and the longer she stayed in Atmore the larger the specter of the other woman loomed in her imagination. As the months piled up, so did Willie Mae's demands on Foster Hale's time and pocketbook. She never would believe he was broke. After all, hadn't he just shelled out thousands to a measly head shrinker? Maybe if she broke him completely, the other woman would desert him. Then her beloved Foster would be all hers. It had taken two decades but at last Willie Mae Clausen was going to get her man. And she was going to get him by breaking him completely . . . financially and emotionally.

Foster Hale began receiving a barrage of phone calls, letters, telegrams. Occasionally, she would visit his office to play on his sympathy. Through all of this, Foster maintained his composure, pledged his love constantly but he just didn't have the money. In his last letter, he had pleaded, "I am old, tired, sick . . . have mercy. . . ." But Willie Mae would have no mercy, not until she had broken her man.

On the morning of June 16, 1931, she sent her last telegram: "Foster . . . urgent send $35 . . . Please. . . ." Foster Hale groaned when he received the message. He didn't have $35. He didn't even have 35 cents but he went to a close friend, borrowed the money and wired it immediately. Willie Mae never received the money, however. While she was waiting for his answer, something snapped in her mind and again she saw the other woman. This time, the other woman was even younger and prettier than Willie Mae ever imagined. She was alive and breathing deeply with a tantalizing smile on her pretty, young lips.

Willie Mae left the telegraph office in a rush, hopped in a borrowed automobile and sped to Mobile where she checked in at the Bienville Hotel. Now she was standing before the desk of the great love of her life, Foster K. Hale, Attorney-at-Law.

"But I sent the money," Foster was saying. "I sent it as soon as I got the telegram." Willie Mae glared down at him, her eyes flashing in rage.

"You're a damned liar!" she said. "You're a two-tim-ing bastard. You gave it to that other woman."

"What other woman?" asked Foster Hale. Then he reached for something in his drawer, perhaps a check, perhaps the stub from the wire, perhaps . . . Willie Mae reached for something, too. She looked in her purse and pulled out a .38 calibre pistol. Foster Hale saw the pistol, stood up, was reaching forward, pleading. . . . Then the gun went off, one shot, then two, then another, and the body of a man slumped forward on the desk, rolled over and made a thud as it hit the floor.

Down on St. Michael Street, two policemen heard the shots. Instantly, they ran to investigate. Just as the police-men were about to charge through the door they heard the soft, tender sobbing of a woman. When they walked into the room they saw in a pool of blood the form of a woman draped across the body of a dead man they had once known as Foster Hale.

When court convened in January, 1932, the trial was long overdue. Willie Mae Clausen had been in the Mobile County jail seven long months; angrily embittered, she had resigned herself to reality, had banished from her tortured mind the memory of her dead lover. The trial had been postponed three times due to the illness of Dis-trict Attorney Bart Chamberlain. Now in January, 1932, she was brought to trial before Judge Joel Goldsby and an hysterical courtroom filled with Mobile women. Cham-berlain asked for death in the electric chair while Willie Mae's attorney, Sam Johnston, pleaded not guilty by rea-son of insanity.

In support of the insanity plea, Sam Johnston brought to the stand the celebrated psychiatrist from New Or-leans, Dr. C.S. Holbrook, then a psychiatrist from Phoe-nix, Arizona, and one from Johns Hopkins in Baltimore.

They were unanimous in their feeling that Willie Mae Clausen suffered from acute paranoia. Then Bart Chamberlain subpoenaed Austill Pharr, later president of the First National Bank. Pharr brought a long bundle of love letters dating from 1922 which had been deposited in the First National Bank. In eloquent pleas, Bart Chamberlain pinned the terms "fading flower" and "gold digger" on the accused woman.

The climactic hour came when Willie Mae herself took the stand. Throughout her testimony she was clearly in an hysterical frame of mind, sobbing at times, crying out loud. Before it was over she had fainted and had to be carried out of the courtroom three times. She was such a pitiable figure on the witness stand and Sam Johnston made such an eloquent summation that when the jury went out it was thought she would certainly be acquitted. When the jury deliberated for five hours with no decision, the supposition was further strengthened. The next day the jury talked it over for eight hours, then filed back into the courtroom.

The reading of the verdict brought forth a demonstration never before witnessed in a Mobile courtroom. Hundreds of women spectators who had brought boxed lunches and hot coffee every day of the trial rose and cheered when Willie Mae Clausen was charged with second degree manslaughter and sentenced to one year in the county jail.

Throughout the trial, Willie Mae's heart-rending contention had been that for twenty-two years she had been in love with the same man, but that he had all these years been merely stringing her along; that he never really loved her and had finally set off the explosion in her mind by jilting her for another woman. The jury must certainly have been touched by all this soul-baring testimony and perhaps Willie Mae would have gotten off scot-free had it not been for the final bit of evidence offered by Bart Chamberlain.

"Was it not true," asked the D.A., "that over a period of twenty-two years Foster Hale gave you a total of $70,000 in addition to an automobile and other items?"

Willie Mae was vague in answering but subsequent evidence showed that this was true. It was the next bit of evidence that proved the shocker, though.

"Do you know anything about a will?" asked Bart Chamberlain.

"No," replied Willie Mae.

"Then," said Chamberlain, "I wish to submit the evidence that when Foster Hale's will was probated, it was discovered that he left half of everything he owned to Willie Mae Clausen." A hush pervaded the courtroom and Willie Mae buried her face in her hands.

The unfortunate lover was inconsolable as she was led off to the county jail. But not for long. In a few weeks, she had succeeded in seducing the jailer. The jailer's own brother, Frank Pryor, was forced to dismiss him from service but when Willie Mae finally was set free, there was Dewitt Pryor, the jailer, waiting patiently. Dewitt and Willie Mae were married soon after and the couple went away to Birmingham. A few months later Frank Pryor received a phone call from a friend in Birmingham telling him that poor Dewitt had lost his wits and that somebody had better come after him. Dewitt Pryor was brought back to Mobile to obtain a divorce and Willie Mae was off to the races again.

Twelve years later, Sam Johnston was sitting in his law office when a heavily made-up woman came bouncing in the door with an armload of jewels dangling from her wrists. Willie Mae was back in town! This time with a new last name to add to her collection. Calling her former attorney to the window, she pointed out a shiny new automobile across the street. As she walked out the door, she mentioned that she had recently married a well-to-do Englishman and was just passing through Mobile on a vacation.

Nobody heard much from Willie Mae after that. A few years ago, Frank Pryor received word that she was living in Pensacola but he didn't catch the name of her latest husband. That she had one, there was no doubt, for whatever she was, Willie Mae was not without.

Chapter 20

Mr. Bellingrath's Gardens

South of Mobile a pleasant little river winds its way into the bay, emanating from the rolling hills a few miles further north. The French named it "Riviere de Isle-aux-Oises", but Mobilians know it as "Fowl River".

Just before Fowl River reaches the Bay of Mobile, it slips around a few choice acres known to millions of tourists from all over the world as Bellingrath Gardens—Charm Spot of the Deep South. These acres were fertile even in the days of the French and Indians, low and swampy, covered with rich, black dirt. Here the oaks grew tall and offered an inviting perch for the varieties of birds that stopped to rest awhile. Below the moss-covered oaks a rich variety of flowers, despite encroachments from weeds, grew wildly into full bloom. This charm spot was just as it had always been when a visit by a man from Mobile changed the flow of its history.

Walter Bellingrath had come to Mobile just after the

turn of the century. Son of a German immigrant, he grew up in Atlanta before migrating to Alabama in 1880. When he was barely seventeen, Bellingrath went to work as a telegraph operator for the L & N Railroad. Moving to Montgomery, he entered the brokerage business and after a moderate success, acquired the franchise to an up-and-coming soda pop business.

It was Coca Cola that made Walter Bellingrath his millions but when he came to Mobile in 1904, hardly anyone had heard of the drink. Bellingrath went to work to turn his product into the most famous drink in the world. He drove his own truck, coined his own slogans, and staged such publicity campaigns that people from Atlanta to New Orleans couldn't get thirsty without thinking of Coca Cola. The result of it all was that he made a fortune and became Mobile's biggest citizen. He helped organize the Waterman Steamship Corporation, the world's largest. He started more corporations, became director for a bank, a newspaper, and a multitude of ware-housing companies. Then he got religious and became one of the pillars of the temple. Financially secure, his thoughts finally turned to philanthropy to which he devoted the rest of his life.

In the midst of all his frantic activity, Walter Bellingrath had met a girl, a home-grown Mobile girl. Her name was Bessie May Morse and her passion was flowers. The prosperous Mr. Bellingrath married Bessie May and shortly was caught up in her enchantment with flowers. In 1917, he went to his Fowl River fishing camp to enjoy a weekend. Looking around the grounds, "Mr. Bell" peered more deeply into the land he had just purchased. It was beautiful, exquisite almost. But there were some flaws, too. The flowers grew wild, untrimmed and un-nourished, fighting a constant battle against weeds and pests. "Maybe God needs a little help," he mused.

When he approached Bessie May with his thoughts, she took some of the azaleas from their Mobile home and transplanted them to Fowl River. They grew even better there so she took some more. Then she took some camellias, then some poinsettias. Soon Bellingrath lost interest in his fishing and began to think more of his flowers. The dream began to take form. He would build a garden, a huge private garden, perhaps the most extensive private garden in the world.

The Bellingraths went to Europe in 1927. They visited the Royal Gardens in England and the most renowned estates in France, Austria, and Germany. Charged with a new ambition for their own gardens, the Bellingraths returned to Mobile with plans for expansion of the Fowl River grounds. Hundreds of new flowers, poinsettas, golden rods, oleanders, chrysanthemums and others, took root and added to the luster of the growing garden.

It was about this time that Bellingrath met a fascinating botanist and gentleman who through the years greatly aided him in the planning and planting of the gardens. "Doctor Loding" was his name. Born in Denmark in 1869, he early developed an interest in botany and entomology. As a young man he went to England, met Queen Victoria, and worked in the Royal Gardens at Kew. After his tenure at Kew, Doctor Loding sailed to America and managed a banana plantation in Nicaragua. Tiring of bananas, he caught a steamer to New York; but on the way north, the ship stopped at Mobile and Loding wandered into *Karl's Place* for a beer. There he met some Germans who spoke as highly of Mobile as they did of beer. The more beer Loding drank, the more he liked Mobile. By the time the ship was ready to debark he was in love with the Port City. He dashed out the door, ran up the gangplank, and retrieved his gear just in time to avoid having to swim back to the docks. Dr. Loding, after roaming the earth, was in Mobile to stay.

The good Doctor's passion was azaleas. He developed new varieties and planted them all over town. Then he started something that was later to be known as the Azalea Trail. After that, he developed the beautiful Watermelon Crepe Myrtle and several other varieties. Besides flowers, Dr. Loding loved trees. He started a city wide campaign to preserve the oaks and saved some revered old magnolias by importing beetles from California that devoured the pests that were eating the magnolias away. After seeing these beetles in action, the Doctor became fascinated with beetles in general and began combing the woods in Saraland, Satsuma, Chunchula and Whistler. When he had finished, Dr. Loding owned one of the foremost beetle collections in the world.

With the help of Dr. Loding and numerous others, Bellingrath, by 1932, had built one of the most elaborate private gardens in America. It was in that year that he decided to invite the general public to visit the grounds. The Bellingraths were totally unprepared for the response that followed. Over the years, word had leaked out to the populace of the splendor of these mysterious gardens. Now that Mobilians at last had a chance to see for themselves, they weren't going to let the opportunity slip by. They came in droves on a Sunday afternoon, jamming the roads and crowding the gates. The people were so enthusiastic about the flowers that the Bellingraths decided that henceforth the grounds would always be open to the general public. At an admission price, of course.

With new vigor, Bellingrath began to think of new improvements. His staff increased, too. Frank Woodward, his Negro fishing companion, had been with him for years. When the gardens went public, Frank became the official greeter and general flunky. In 1934, Bellingrath hired a general manager and landscape artist named A. A. Hunt. The talented Hunt had, like Loding, had worked at the Royal Gardens at Kew. Besides being a horticulturist and Bellingrath's general manager, Hunt was a valuable public relations man. He stumped all over America making speeches about the gardens, always ending his talks the same way.

"Buildings and streets," he would say, "commence to deteriorate the moment they are built; but the glories of nature exemplified in her flowers go on, always giving that something to the human soul that voice nor pen can describe."

Today Bellingrath Gardens has pushed out and away from the few small acres that once huddled around the bluff on Fowl River. The Gardens property consists of eight hundred acres with nearly sixty-five of them landscaped. Visitors come the year around to walk on the flagstone paths. These flagstones which once paved the streets of Mobile were brought to this country originally as ballast for ships arriving in Mobile Bay. Tourists walking these paths in the fall find an abundance of camellia japonicas lining the walkways, just beginning to open their petals for a parade which reaches full bloom during the wintertime. When the japonicas have gone to sleep, the azaleas awaken to take their place, reaching their full glory in February or March. After the azaleas have retired for the season, the mountain laurels and the dogwoods branch out with a softer, less brilliant display of beauty. The summer tourists enjoy the crepe myrtles and hydrangeas, as well as the myriad shrubs and plants which cover the woodlands.

One of the paths leads directly to the Bellingrath

home which stands majestically in the middle of the gardens. Upon entering the front portals, one is immediately struck by the charm of the design and construction, the richness of the furnishings and the rarity of the *"objets d'art"* that adorn the living room and dining room. The porcelain and china collections are, indeed, a marvel of priceless antiques, gathered from over the world by Mrs. Belllingrath.

The flower of Mr. Bellingrath's life passed away in 1943. Bessie May had been his chief source of inspiration since the early days when together they had dreamed of creating the gardens. Now the dream had been fulfilled and his partner in the dream was gone.

For the next twelve years, Walter Bellingrath walked the paths of his gardens alone. Strolling through the forests in the early morning light, the lean, white-haired octogenarian would stop to examine his beloved plants. Then, whistling a sad hillbilly tune, he would move on down the trail to another scenic wonder, just around the next bend. He rounded the last bend in 1955, leaving behind a wondrous legacy as a monument of his life-long belief in the power of beauty to uplift the soul.

"My flowers are my friends," Mr. Bellingrath used to say, "and among my friends I feel closer to God."

Chapter 21

Femmes, Flowers, and Frolics

Frolicking has always occupied a prominent place in the life of Mobilians. The islands, the beaches and the bayous offer as wide a variety of sporting events as any place in America.

Before the twentieth century, fishing and sailboat racing were the most popular events. In recent years, however, ice follies, organized sports and stock car racing have horned in on the water sports. Even the water sports have become more sophisticated, though. Back in 1929, the first Deep Sea Fishing Rodeo took place on Dauphin Island and brought out 250 sportsmen. It was a little rough in those days. A bridge to Dauphin Island was only a dream and even when the sportsmen got there, there was no place to stay except in the old brick barracks of Fort Gaines. But these few rough and ready souls started the rodeo off and had themselves a whale of a fishing party. Today, the fishing party is bigger and better than ever. The building of the Dauphin Island

Bridge made it possible for everybody to attend and now sportsmen come in droves from all over the globe to match fish hooks and poles with the crowds. Records of the sizes and various types of salt water fish are kept at rodeo headquarters. When the competition is over, valuable prizes are awarded to the fish-catchers. Most of the early records have been broken in recent years, although old timers like to say, "The fish ain't what they used to be." What they probably mean is that the "fish stories" ain't the same. In at least one case, they have a point. Back in 1936, Tom Twitty landed a prize tarpon that weighed 139 pounds 8 ounces. Nobody needed a "fish story" to describe that one; the record still stands.

Visitors to Mobile Bay are astounded by a phenomenon known to Alabamians as "Jubilee." Marine biologists are equally astounded when they see what seems to be half the Gulf's fish running aground near Point Clear on the Bay's eastern shore. At the first cry of "Jubilee!" the residents are running down to the seashore with buckets and nets. For hours, while the fish are lying languidly in the sun, the people are busy scooping them up by the thousands and carting them off. Jubilee is an infrequent visitor to Mobile Bay and it comes without warning; but for a few brief hours the community is electrified with excitement.

Sailboating is almost a year-round affair but football comes but once a year. When it does, the city is alive with pigskin talk. Of course, Mobile has enjoyed football just about as long as any other city but it only hit the big time in 1948. In that year, the Mobile Touchdown Club was formed and the Ernest F. Ladd Memorial Stadium was host to its first collegiate game. Three years later the Senior Bowl Game came to Mobile to stay and gave Mobilians the chance to see some of the greatest names in football. Most of today's greatest professional stars ended their collegiate careers by participating in the Senior Bowl. Back in 1958, against National Champion Louisiana State University, the legendary Bear Bryant started off his great career at Alabama with a bang. He walked into Ladd Stadium, raised his hand and the end zone bleachers fell in.

Before the advent of collegiate football, baseball was the big thing in organized sports. The Mobile Bears convened at Hartwell Field, named after the illustrious mayor, Harry Hartwell. As a farm club for the old Brooklyn Dodgers, the Bears developed a covey of exciting players who later went on to the majors. Among the Bear heroes were Gordy Coleman, Don Zimmer, Chuck Conners and Jim Gentile. There were others, too, Billy Kerr, Ray Shearer, Frank and Milton Bolling. The man Mobilians got most excited over, though, was their slugger, George "Shotgun" Shuba who poled many a ball over the right field fence, before moving up to Ebbetts Field in Brooklyn.

Hartwell Field is still there but the Bears have gone into permanent hibernation. The stadium now plays host to such events as the annual October fair which brings into Mobile a carnival of amusement thrills, glittering lights and vivacious girls.

The girls have always gotten special attention around Mobile, ever since the days of Madame Le Vert and Margaret Lea. Margaret was the pretty young thing who was staying at the home of William Bledsoe in Spring Hill when visited by the gallant General Sam Houston. Romance was the last thing on the minds of the Bledsoes and the Leas. It was not so much the difference in ages (he was 47 and she was 21) but the incongruity in temperament and background. Houston was a hard-drinking frontiersman, loudly profane, more accustomed to fighting Indians and Mexicans than chatting on the gallery. Besides, he was a divorced man and an unlikely suspect for remarriage. Margaret Lea was exactly the opposite. Dainty, devoutly religious and sheltered, she was in absolute awe of the great Texan.

But Sam Houston was smitten the first night they walked in the Bledsoe Gardens. After a week under the Mobile sky, the General was completely caught up with the charm of Margaret in the romantic atmosphere of old Mobile. After a week, the General left Alabama but he came back later to marry Margaret and she followed him to Texas where together they rode into the full sunlight of a greater glory.

Another Mobile belle came along a few years after the Civil War. Her name was Eoline Eilands and she lived in the grand mansion on St. Emanuel Street. A comely young girl, she attracted the attentions of a sailor and fell madly in love with him. He promised to marry her as soon as he came back from his next voyage and Eoline dressed up in her finest Victorian garments to meet him at the docks on the appointed day. His ship didn't come in that day but Eoline waited until the next day, then the next week, then . . . sixty years later, she was still waiting. When she was past eighty years of age, she would dress up in her decorous but outlandish costume and take her morning stroll down to the docks to see if the ship had come in. With her long skirts spread out and dragging the ground, and with her smooth, even gait, she seemed to be moving along without any apparent motivation. She would glide down the streets like a daylight ghost with her long, flowing hair floating softly in the breeze. She would sail past a group of boys playing baseball and the game would halt at once while the young players stared in amazement at the haunting figure of a woman floating past them. "Floating Eiland," they called her as did everyone else in Mobile. "Floating Eiland" made an indelible impression on everyone who ever saw her. She was in the world of Mobilians for many, many years but she was never really in their world at all. For sixty years, she went her own proud little way, clutching fiercely to the past, her soul secure against the encroachments of time, her memories tucked safely inside her devout little heart.

Another of the fabulous belles of Mobile was and is Madame Rose Palmai-Tenser. Called the "Rose of the South," by the Metropolitan Opera House, the Madame was an opera singer in Czechoslavakia when she met and married a lumberman. When Hitler moved into Czechoslavakia, Madame Rose and her husband fled to England where she became a nurse. Sailing to the New World, Madame Rose's husband smelled the pine resin of Mobile County and the couple came to the port city to stay. It was fortunate for music-loving Mobilians that they did. Madame Rose became a singing teacher at Spring Hill, then founded the Opera Guild and staged Mobile's first grand opera. In 1958, the Madame's cultural pursuits were duly recognized when she was named First Lady of the Year.

After years of being in the background the Mobile belles finally grabbed the national spotlight. Vickie Powers, a graduate of Murphy High School and a former student of Madame Rose, won the Miss Alabama title, easily captured the talent contest at Atlantic City, then went on to Broadway and the Metropolitan Opera.

A few years before, another one of Madame Rose's pupils became the first Alabamian to win the Miss America title. Yolande "Bebe" Betbeze walked across the judges platform in 1951 and presented such a ravishing picture of beauty that the judges could have foregone the other preliminaries. After a month of touring,

"Bebe" came home to a welcome not given to any Mobile belle since Madame Le Vert. Thirty thousand frantic fans received her at Ladd Stadium in an exuberant ceremony that Mobilians would long remember. After a brief career in show business "Bebe" married the film producer, Mathew M. Fox and has since lived in New York City. She returned to Mobile in 1951 to appear before 15,000 people packed in Bienville Square. The occasion was a ceremony that has become nationally famous in itself—the Azalea Trail.

Back in 1929, acting on an idea by Sam Lackland, a Mobile businessman, the Junior Chamber of Commerce began encouraging Mobilians to plant azaleas as a tourist attraction. When the first new crop bloomed, the Jaycees began distributing literature inviting the public to drive along the avenues and winding roads through the heart of the residential section. Legend has it that Fifise Langlois brought the first azaleas to Mobile during the eighteenth century. The legend may be true but it was the Mobile Jaycees who gave the planting project the big boost it needed and organized the ceremonies that led up to the grand event—the Azalea Trail Pageant, where one of Mobile's high school senior girls is chosen to reign over the Azalea Trail Festival. The annual event is now held in the Mobile Municipal Auditorium and the finals are televised. On that night, the Old South comes to life again as the young beauties parade before the camera in their brilliant ante-bellum laces.

The Jaycees also sponsor the Junior Miss Pageant which selects the most charming and outstanding high school senior girl in the nation. Coinciding with the azalea season, the Junior Miss Pageant is held in late February or early March and is now nationally televised in color and emceed each year by a popular television personality.

The Azalea Trail begins beneath the spreading branches of the moss-covered oaks in the heart of the city. Moving westward along Government Street, the trail winds its way past ante-bellum homes and quaint patios for seventeen miles through the city's residential areas. Driving down the trail, visitors can see some of the famous old homes which stand near the azaleas— the Fort Condé-Charlotte House at the site of the first great fort in the Louisiana Territory; the historical old Quigley Home, now the Jaycee headquarters; the Maury Home, the Admiral Semmes Home and the Richards House. Then comes the fabulous Oakleigh, now head-quarters for the Mobile Historical Preservation Society. Begun in 1833 on the highest point of what was known as Simon Favre's old Spanish land grant, the home was not fully completed until twenty years later by James W. Roper. Built by slave labor, Oakleigh came to be recognized as Mobile's official ante-bellum home. With its winding staircase, its square columns, its exquisite set-ting, the home hosted some of the leading personalities of the pre-war era—people like Madame Le Vert and President William Henry "Tippecanoe" Harrison. Several relics of the Walton-Le Vert family still remain at Oak-leigh, including the Thomas Sully portrait of Madame Le Vert.

Further on down the trail is the elegant Mitchell Home on Spring Hill Avenue. More popularly known as "The Bragg Home," it was built by John Bragg and later willed to his brother, Confederate General Braxton Bragg.

The trail covers many other resplendent old homes— the Craft Home, Jordon Place, the Acker Home, and innumerable others.

Near the end of the line close to Spring Hill College one comes to the most interesting of all—Yester House.

Built in the 1830's by William Dawson, Yester House was adapted from the Tower of the Winds of ancient Greece. Complementing its strange beauty are the hidden chambers on the grounds and the legends of hidden treasure, ghosts and the purported hiding place of the Copeland Gang. In this century alone no less than three ghosts have been reported by responsible witnesses.

It is true that a young woman was hanged—some say accidentally—during the construction of the building. For years afterwards, neighborhood residents saw the spectre of a young woman dancing on the front lawn as though she were dangling from the end of a rope.

When Mr. and Mrs. William C. Perdue moved into the house in 1955, most folks had forgotten about the ghosts. One day Mrs. Perdue and two friends were outside on the lawn trying to figure out how to get into the locked house. Suddenly the eyes of Mrs. Perdue's friends brightened. "The young woman upstairs will let us in," they said. "She was just staring out the window."

Mrs. Perdue's face clouded. "Nonsense," she exclaimed. "That window's seven feet from the floor." But the two witnesses persisted in their story, one even going so far as to draw a picture of the young woman. Even Mrs. Perdue's mother, a no-nonsense woman herself, later claimed she saw the ghosts at least three times.

Then there was the man in the backyard electrocuted by lightning during a thunderstorm with his hands on the iron fence. Since that time, every thunderstorm brings reports of a man struggling frantically to free himself from the fence of iron.

Typical ghost stories, perhaps. But yet unexplained are more tangible mysteries. Why the huge, underground, waterproof room in the garden under the water fountain? And what about the forty-foot-long, brick tunnel discovered only a few years ago by accident? Was there any connection between the cotton merchant William Dawson and the Copeland Gang? And so go the legends of Yester House, an enchanting blend of Grecian beauty and Mobile mystery.

Chapter 22

Bishop Toolen, Inc.

On Mardi Gras day of 1927, just after Billy Sunday had left town, Mobilians picked up the morning paper to read of the coming of another religious figure. The *Register* said his name was Father Thomas Joseph Toolen of Baltimore and that Pope Pius XI had selected him to fill the vacancy left by the death of Bishop Edward Allen. Then the report went on to describe the appointee in glowing terms.

Bishop Toolen, so read the story, had been born in Baltimore on February 28, 1886, one of six children of Thomas Toolen and Mary Dowd, both natives of Ireland. At the age of twelve, young Toolen announced that he would like to be a priest but his mother was not certain he had the call. Maybe the young boy was just impressed by his older brother William, a seminary student. At any rate, he went on to Loyola College where he entered St. Mary Seminary and was finally ordained a priest in 1910 by the renowned Cardinal Gibbons.

After ordination, Toolen studied canon law at Catholic University in Washington, D. C., then received his first parish appointment at St. Bernard Church in Baltimore. At St. Bernard, Toolen impressed Archbishop Curley as an organizer in the establishment of Holy Name Units, Sodalities, Dramatic Clubs and Boy Scout troops. Later he became Propagation Director and succeeded in raising large sums of money which he personally presented to Pope Pius XI. Then his appointment to the bishopric of Mobile came.

The Mobile Register had expressed hope in an editorial that Mardi Gras morning that "Father Toolen will find the Mobile bishopric a pleasant and profitable field for his labors." The words were prophetic and the hopes of the editor went far beyond expectations. Bishop Toolen blew into Mobile like a northern cyclone and set to work in a whirlwind of energy to build up the diocese. A few days after his arrival, he went out to Spring Hill to look over the college where his five predecessors had spent so much of their time and energy. It was here that Bishop Michael Portier, the first Bishop of Mobile, had founded the great institution in 1830. On the eve of the Civil War Bishop Portier died and Bishop John Quinlan led the good Catholics through the trying days of the war. Then came Bishops Dominic Manucy, J. J. O'Sullivan and finally Bishop Edward Allen who had died the previous October. Looking back on the record of these Bishops, Thomas Toolen must have felt a sense of awe, especially since he was succeeding Bishop Allen after a long, distinguished career that spanned three decades. Little did Thomas Toolen realize then that his own career was to outdistance all of these in length of service and personal achievement. His only concern that day was to lay the cornerstone of the new building called Mobile Hall.

The laying of that cornerstone was the first in a long program of construction that was to eventually gain for the bishop the title of "The Builder." Surveying his diocese in 1927, he found that there were forty-nine counties in Alabama without a Catholic Church of any kind. He promised himself that before he died every county in Alabama would have at least one Catholic mission. By 1967, he had built missions and churches for thirty-two additional counties, which left only seventeen more to be taken care of before he passed on.

But it was not only missions that Bishop Toolen was interested in. Under his direction, there were 112 convents built, 104 parish halls, 23 hospitals, 119 rectories, 17 high schools, 95 grade schools and over 50 other buildings built during his term. Presently, the total stands at just over 700, but the ambitious Bishop surely has his eye set on an even thousand before he's through.

How has a spiritual leader, a man most folks usually regard lightly insofar as business acumen is concerned, managed to stir up such enthusiasm for a building program? His close associates agree that Bishop Toolen is a past master at the art of raising money. "If the bishop hadn't gone into religion," they say, "he would have been a millionaire." And then some people say that he really is a millionaire, anyway, and that he owns half of Dauphin Street. So go the stories that have built the bishop into a legend in his own diocese. Over the years he has received enough honors to choke an elephant. Loyola, Spring Hill, and a host of other universities have given him honorary degrees. The National Holy Name Society awarded him its highest award for a bishop, the Shield of B. I. Gregory X, Crusader. In 1961, Italy bestowed on him the award for commander of Order of Merit. The next year, Lebanon give him the Order of Cedars Medal. And in 1965, he received the St. Peter Claver

Medal for services to the Negro. This, in spite of the fact that the venerable bishop is somewhat of a conservative and loudly condemns disorderly racial demonstrations.

One of the bishop's warmest admirers has always been George Wallace. When Wallace was elected Governor, he almost decided to make the bishop a colonel but the Bishop decided one title was enough. Instead, the Governor awarded him a certificate of appreciation and a plaque on the occasion of Toolen's eightieth birthday.

The bishop's biggest day came in 1960. The mayor of Mobile proclaimed Bishop Toolen Day in the port city to honor the fiftieth anniversary of Toolen's ordination. It wasn't just a Mobile celebration, however. Catholics all over the country joined in the well-wishing. Cardinal Cushing came to Mobile as did Bishop Fulton J. Sheen. There were parades, pageants and banquets all the week of the Golden Jubilee Anniversary. Besides a groundbreaking ceremony on site of the new St. Mary's Home, there was a civic reception and a testimonial dinner, then finally the chief religious event of the celebration—the Pontifical Mass of Thanksgiving.

Today, at 82, Bishop Toolen directs the diocese with a steady hand. His eyes still have the color of baby blue and his snowy white hair gives him an appearance of saintliness. And he still has that roly-poly physique and the boundless energy for which he is noted. He likes to travel and he does plenty of it, 50,000 miles a year, to be exact. Every summer for the past 30 years, he has gone back to Ireland where his parents were born and where many of his relatives still live. Sometimes, he travels to Rome where in times past he has conferred with the Popes, Pius, John and Paul. He also buzzes around the United States, making hundreds of public speeches every year.

"How do I do it?" he asks, and then answers, "The Lord lets me do it and as long as the Lord is willing, I shall continue going and going."

He still travels a lot, too, on the back roads of his diocese to the little churches he helped spring into existence. It's a lot different now than when he first came to Alabama. There weren't very many paved roads then and the backwoods Protestants took a dim view of his invasion of their territory. The Bishop likes to tell the story of what happened to him years ago when he was in a railroad depot in a little country town waiting on a train. One of his community priests was standing at the depot with him and the two of them were objects of curiosity. The townsfolk were gaping at their religious garb.

"They all heard you were in town," whispered the priest to Bishop Toolen. "They only think I have horns but they're absolutely certain that you do."

The bishop looked around at the curious bystanders. Then he took off his hat and smiled, as if to prove that he had no horns. Finally, one of the stunned villagers spoke up. "Well, I be dog," he gasped. "He ain't got none, yet, anyway."

Protestant skepticism has fallen by the wayside since that time. At least as far as personal relationships are concerned. The genial Bishop counts almost as many friends from other denominations as he does from his own. He delights in talking to visitors from other cities, taking them to his beloved Basilica of the Immaculate Conception, and pointing out the tombs of the former Bishops who lie beneath the Basilica floor. Then he proudly points to the vault where one day the sixth Bishop will be laid to rest. Good-naturedly, he mentions that he is hopeful that won't be too soon. He has far too much to do to think about resting.

In his own lifetime, Bishop Toolen is already an institution and his niche is securely etched in the history of Mobile. The institution has been based on duty, unselfishness and love for his fellow man. Perhaps what Bishop Toolen loves most in this life is children. He, himself, said it once when he was commended for the great work he had done in establishing orphanages for the homeless. "I not only love orphans," said the great man, "I love all children. And that's when I'm the happiest— when I'm right in the middle of them."

Chapter 23

Mardi Gras Time

It was a dismal day in February in the year 1866. A blanket of gloom yet hung heavy in the air over Mobile. The War had been over for nearly a year but Mobilians were still lost in self-pity. They sat around their stores and homes doing as little as they could get away with. A few Union soldiers walked the streets passing the time as best they could. Nobody was having any fun.

Then one of the soldiers thought he heard the sound of a drum. He turned and saw a weird sight. An Indian chief outfitted in all his trimmings was sitting on top of a charcoal wagon, yelling and waving a pair of drumsticks. As the horse-drawn wagon rolled up Dauphin Street, the soldiers could see six more Indians sitting in the back of the wagon. They were likewise yelling and waving rattles, beating on tin cans and singing to the top of their lungs. When the wagon reached Bienville Square, the shocked troops had recovered. Now their suspicions were aroused. Could this be part of a Confederate plot to seize the city? The troops went for their guns and took positions behind the oak trees.

"Halt!" the Sergeant of the Guards yelled. He raised his hand, then walked up to the wagon. The Indian Chief pulled on the reins and stood up straight in the wagon.

"Who are you?" asked the sergeant, while his eyes glanced suspiciously at the wagon, searching for guns or explosives.

"I am Chief Slacabamorinico," said the wild-eyed driver. The sergeant looked at him blankly.

"Stepped in what?" he said.

"Slacabamorinico," replied the driver, "Chief of the Chickasaws."

"Oh," said the Sergeant, "that's what I thought you said."

Then the chief sat back down. The soldiers came out from behind the trees and walked up to where the sergeant stood scratching his head.

"What're they doing?" asked one soldier.

"Just raisin' hell," said the sergeant.

The hell-raising chieftain was Joe Cain, an exuberant roustabout who had just come from New Orleans where he had witnessed a Mardi Gras parade. Mobilians hadn't seen a Mardi Gras parade in so long they had almost forgotten such a thing existed. But on the day that Joe Cain dressed up as a Chickasaw Indian and led his small band of followers all over the city streets, Mardi Gras was born again and Mobile hasn't been quite the same since.

Joe Cain didn't originate Mardi Gras; he only revived it. The celebration had been started when one Nicholas Langlois established the Société de la Sainte Louis in 1704 back when Mobile was up the river. The Indians soon took up the idea and started their own Mardi Gras celebration. Then Mobile moved down river and Langlois with his friends and the sanction of Bienville started a celebration which they called *Boeuf Gras*. Taking a huge effigy of a bull's head, they marched up and down Dauphin and Royal streets and stirred up a parade. Years later the descendants of these Frenchmen imported a giant bull's head from France. It took twenty men to lift it off the ground and place it on a carriage pulled by oxen. During the Civil War, the filling in the bull's head was used as wadding for the cannons which defended Mobile. Out of this practice, came the expression "shootin' the bull."

When the Spanish came, they started their own mystic societies. The English didn't get too excited about it all but the Americans added a little ingenuity to the frolicking. All these celebrations, however, were rather small and only a few of the more robust citizens participated. It remained for a young Mobilian named Michael Krafft to really get the show on the road. On the night of December 31, 1830, Krafft was dining with a dozen or so friends in Antoine La Tourette's cafe at the corner of Water and Conti Streets. Just before midnight, the party left the restaurant and came to Partridge's hardware store. Feeling chipper after an evening of guzzling the water of life, they seized the hoes, rakes and cowbells that stood in front of the store. Thus armed, they began a parade that lasted until everybody in town was awakened. They paraded up to the mayor's doorstep and that good-natured official invited them in for more refreshments. The whole affair was pronounced a

great success. The next year the Krafft group added another dozen members to its exclusive society and they
called themselves the *Midnight Revelers*. By 1834, they
were wearing masks and costumes and had adopted the
name *Cowbellion de Rakin Society*. *The Tea-Drinkers
Society* organized in 1844 and over the next decade and
a half, the celebration gradually increased in intensity.
By 1861, it was defunct. The able-bodied men had all
gone off to war. Over the next five years, the celebration
of Boeuf Gras was all but forgotten.

But Joe Cain had, in 1866, brought Boeuf Gras back
to the minds of the public. All the year following the appearance of Slacabamorinico, Joe Cain's antics were the
talk of Mobile. In the midst of despair, it was the one
thing Mobilians could get excited about. On the next
Shrove Tuesday, Joe Cain reappeared on the streets of
Mobile, this time as the leader of a company of sixteen
ex-Confederates who called themselves the Lost Cause
Minstrels. By this time, Joe Cain had enlisted the support
of some of the most prominent members of the community such as editor John Cothran, and Judge Oliver
J. Semmes. Mardi Gras in Mobile was off and running.

Inspired by Cain, other societies sprang into action:
the *Order of the Myths,* the *Infant Mystics*, the *Knights
of Revelry*. In 1872, a carnival association was formed
and created an emperor whose name was to go ringing
forever through the years—Felix!

The legend behind the Felix parade was that Mobile,
the capital of a vast empire, was ruled by a great poten-
tate who bore that happy name. The extent of his empire was so great that Felix could only visit his beloved
city once a year. At high noon on Shrove Monday, his
ship would come gliding over the waters of Mobile Bay.

Entering the city, he was wildly received by his subjects and was given full homage until midnight of Shrove Tuesday, when he disappeared across the ocean for another year.

The legend of King Felix became so popular that five years later New Orleans copy-catted the idea, calling its emperor King Rex. The first Felix was Daniel E. Huger. Then follows a long list of prominent Mobilians who have worn the purple—T.C. De Leon, John Rapier, Peter Alba, and Alfred Staples. It was the colorful Alfred Lewis Staples who became the successor to Joe Cain as a leading spirit of Mardi Gras. Descendant of that early Mobile colonist, Jean-Baptiste Baudreau de la Graveline, genial Mr. Staples was such a staunch promoter of the carnival that he gained the title "Mr. Mardi Gras." He was King in 1916 and for fifty years thereafter was the guiding spirit of the festival.

Scores of societies have been organized in the years since Joe Cain got the wagon rolling. *The Strikers* reactivated their old unit of the 1840's; then came the *Dragons,* the *Desconocides,* the *Crewe of Columbus,* the *Fifty Funny Fellows,* the *Stripers,* the *Polka Dots* and the *Comic Cowboys.*

The Cowboys launched their first parade in 1884, spurred on by the energetic bubble of mirth, Dave Levi. For forty years, little Dave lived and breathed the Comic Cowboy parade. He was about his plans all year, sometimes hopping out of bed at four A.M. to jot down ideas. He was constantly devising and revising skits and schemes for his belly-busting floats. It was no wonder, then, that the parade of the Comic Cowboys was always the most eagerly awaited procession. It was funny, hilariously funny; the first parade had been a burlesque called, "Dr. Cutter's Wildest Westest Show." It was a take-off on the glories of Western life, replete with ridiculous cowhands and innocuous Indians, sad-faced and pot-bellied. It was the funniest thing Mobile had ever seen and Dave Levi spent the rest of his life trying to beat it. He did take-offs on presidents, doctors, circuses, elections, even angels. When he died in 1925, the Cowboys lost their guiding hand, their boss cowboy. But within a few years they regained a sense of humor and have ever since been regaling their rabid supporters.

Today Mardi Gras in Mobile generates more excitement than ever. The tourists see only the parades but Mobilians think of Mardi Gras as a season, a season of fabulous masquerade balls that lead up to the grand finale of parades. The dances begin well before Christmas with the Strikers ball closing out the year in the most elaborate manner. All through January and February scores of dances are given by the respective societies, reaching a breathtaking crescendo of activity during the last week. Then Felix arrives on the Monday before Shrove Tuesday and the whirlwind begins. Over the next thirty-six hours no less than six major dances and nine full-length parades swing into action and Mobile is alive with color and gaiety. The Jolly Jesters and the Mystical Belles and all the others move down Government Street in hourly intervals. White horses pound their shoes on the pavement, prancing majestically by the gaping throngs of bug-eyed spectators. The blasts of clarions are heard in the distance, then suddenly the bands break through the air and the pulse begins to beat more swiftly. The twirlers strut their stuff and the boom-boom-boom of the bass drums strikes cadence with the heart-beat. The first floats come rolling by and waves of children begin to yell with hands out-stretched for the little rubber balls and candies that come sailing through the air.

Then the float is gone, followed by another band. The

children momentarily glance at the adults. But there are no adults. The mature, the aged, the infirm are, for a few ecstatic moments, caught up in the magic of a child's wonderland. A hand reaches out for the prize but the prize eludes it. Now another float is coming! This one is bigger with flashier crepe paper and clowns and more candies. The bands get louder and the crowds noisier. Then the last float passes by and the crowds disperse. But they will be back again. The next parade begins in forty-five minutes. After the last parade by the Order of Myths there is a general letdown. But it doesn't last long. There will always be another one next year, a bigger one and a better one.

Mobilians are not inclined to make the inevitable comparison between New Orleans' Mardi Gras and their own. They don't go all out to impress the tourist. It is more exclusive than that, more like a big, private party, held for the exclusive enjoyment of the greater family of Mobilians. If they thought about it at all, a private conclusion might be, "If theirs is bigger, ours is best."

Chapter 24

Along Davis Avenue

The broad avenue named for Jefferson Davis runs slightly downhill, slanting away from the Mobile business district in a northwest direction toward Toulminville. Sometimes called the "Harlem of Mobile," Davis Avenue means to the Mobilian not just a street but a whole section. Along with Maysville, it is "Colored Mobile."

Near the end of Davis Avenue, on a raised plot of ground, stands an old mansion built just after the turn of the century by one of Mobile's most remarkable Negroes—Dave Patton. This enterprising soul came up just like any other Negro in the late nineteenth century. He gained his bread by the sweat of his brow, working long and hard hours at menial tasks. But Dave Patton was not like the rest of his day-laboring friends. His keen mind was keeping time with the movement of his strong muscles. He thought he saw an opportunity in the contracting business. "You don't need a great deal of capital to get into contracting," he reasoned. "Only a little money and some smart figuring."

If "figuring" was what it took, Dave Patton was sure to do it. With his lightning sharp brain, he could out figure anybody he ever ran across. Noticing one day a batch of goods being transported across town, Dave went to the owner of the goods, told him he could do the same job for less money, and made an offer. Dave didn't get that job but the next time that same man had something to haul, he contacted the resourceful young Patton and made a proposition. Dave Patton shook his head. It wasn't much of an offer and Dave's figuring told him he couldn't so much as break even. Any other businessman would have turned down flat an offer to lose money. But not Dave Patton. He saw more in the deal than a quick profit. He contracted the job, rented some mules and hired the cheapest labor he could find. Cracking the whip on labor and mules, the young contractor finished the job in record time. He barely broke even on his first job, but the important thing was that he had established himself. No longer just another day laborer, Dave Patton was a bona fide hauling contractor. From now on, he would be tougher to deal with.

The next contract Dave Patton got he made a substantial profit, nothing really big but a fair size haul for his second time around. Then the contracts got bigger and covered a greater variety of jobs. He started buying his own mules and wagons; then he got into the demolition business. Before he hauled away the rubbage, he got the contract for tearing down the building. Things were looking up. Dave Patton rented himself an office on Royal Street and hired a couple of secretaries and some full time assistants. He was really up-town, now. Then he got Mardi Gras contracts from most of the Mystic organizations. For the next two decades it would be Dave

Patton's mules and Dave Patton's men at the bottom of every successful parade.

Real estate speculating was a natural for a man of Dave's talents and knowledge. With an uncanny sense of value and a talent for driving hard bargains, Patton made a small fortune buying and selling real estate. Before many years, he had become one of the wealthiest men in Mobile, white or black. Above all, he was proud of the fact that nobody had ever given him anything. What he had, he had earned—by brains, guts and sweat. Now he would become a philanthropist, the first Negro philanthropist in Mobile. He donated land for several public buildings, then he looked around at the colored children playing in the streets on Davis Avenue. He gave the community a number of choice acres; thousands of colored children are still enjoying the playground today.

One day Dave Patton's eyes fell on a peculiar, high strip of land on Davis Avenue. He had noticed it before; indeed, it was hard not to notice it. But this particular day he observed more closely. It was in reality an old battery, one of the many breastworks thrown up by the Confederates during the Civil War to defend Mobile from the Yankees. But the Yankees never came that way, and the breastworks remained for children to scale the heights and to fight mock battles with sticks, clay and stones.

David Patton had always said he wanted nothing but the best. To his mind this battery offered the highest and best location for a home site on Davis Avenue. With his hired help and mules, he attacked the hill with the ferocity of a Union onslaught. In two months he had miraculously cut down the battery to size and had shaped himself a lot which was the envy of everyone on the street. After the landscaping, he began construction of his "dream home." For sheer beauty and symmetry, Dave Patton's two-story mansion rivaled any of the big houses on Government Street. He put some big square columns on the wide front porch and added a colorful tile floor with fancy shingles and an iron gate.

Dave was still a young man when he went to live in his beloved mansion. One day in 1926, he was approached in his Royal Street office by a building contractor. There was a new fad just beginning to sweep the country, the man said. "Talking pictures," people called it and Mobile was going to attract audiences from all over the Gulf Coast with the finest theatre ever built in Alabama. Would Dave be interested in doing the demolition, digging and hauling work involved in laying the foundation the man asked.

Dave Patton was delighted to get the contract for such a history-making theatre. All through the long winter months, he stood in the wet, cold water up to his knees, directing his men and his machines until the old buildings were removed and the foundation holes were dug. Even before the job was completed, a hacking cough came on; slowly at first, then surely over the months till it broke him. After the job was completed, Dave was taken out to Colorado Springs to recuperate. His young wife and a German doctor stayed with him over the long, summer months as he grew weaker and his breathing became more faint. Once he was asked if he wished to go home but he said no, he wouldn't go home in his condition, that he'd always held his head high in Mobile and he didn't want his friends to see him flat on his back.

The end finally came in September, 1927. Dave Patton was rolled back to Mobile on the train and buried at the age of 47. Today, the Widow Patton still lives in the old mansion at 1252 Davis Avenue, a monument to Dave's talent and drive. There is another monument, too, that still stands—a beautiful edifice that, over the years, has brought joy and amusement to all Mobilians—the Saenger Theatre.

There have been other success stories on Davis Avenue. Roger Thomas began his career as a yardman, then became a landscape artist, then a businessman. Before he was through, he bought a large estate with a private swimming pool. When J.L. LeFlore began promoting sit-ins, Thomas invited the public to a dip-in.

Raymond Scott came to Davis Avenue in 1940 and opened a cleaning and pressing shop, then bought a chain of shops. Later, he was elected Mayor of Colored Mobile and became a big promoter of civic affairs.

There are many outstanding Negroes in colored Mobile today. Julius Cook, who won the "Venerable Citizen of the Year" award and W.R.F. Grant, Principal of Booker T. Washington Junior High School; Willie Brown and Rev. C.A. Tunstall, Pastor of the Stone Street Baptist Church, and "Doc" Ortmann who has been passing out drugs on Davis Avenue for longer than anyone can remember. That is, except for his colleague, the man who has been prescribing his drugs for over a half century, Dr. J.A. Franklin.

Dr. Franklin is known to his closest friends as "Chief" partly because he is a natural born leader and partly because he is a full-quarter Indian. Dr. Franklin's mother was born a slave but his father was one of the few free men of color before the Civil War by virtue of Dr. Franklin's grandfather having emigrated from Africa and paid 700 dollars for his wife who was half-Indian and half-Negro.

Besides treating practically every resident in colored Mobile, Dr. Franklin has accumulated a long list of honors and degrees. Reputedly a millionaire, the good doctor is a crackerjack bridge-player and past-president of the Utopia Club. He has seen a multitude of events on the big street but his favorite show is the liveliest event this side of Bourbon Street—the Colored Mardi Gras.

Each year, it begins the same—King Elexis and his Royal Court arrive from the Island of Mirth at the foot of Elmira Street. Met by the Honorable Mayor of Colored Mobile, the procession moves majestically along to Texas Street, thence to Conception, Delaware and Hamilton Streets. When the King and Court reach the Elk's Club, the procession halts for the main ceremony. The King has his tea, then the Queen's Coronation is followed by the presentation of the city's key by the Honorable Mayor. Then the parade runs down Davis Avenue, always orderly, with great dignity but in flamboyant style and flashing colors. When the parade finally reaches Central High School, it comes to a halt and the gala affair is over until the next year.

Mardi Gras livens up Davis Avenue during the carnival season but the street is not exactly dead the rest of the year, especially on Saturday night. Club Savoy and the Ebony Social Club are in full swing on that gay evening and the pendulum is a long-time swinging. During the daytime, Buster's Eagle Pawn Shop is the scene of some real heart-to-heart swapping.

Out of Mobile's Harlem has come some of baseball's greats. Besides Willie McCovey and Tommy Agee, Mobile has contributed one of baseball's all-time greats, who seems to get better with each passing year—the redoubtable Hank Aaron.

Perhaps the greatest player in baseball history came

off the Mobile sandlots. Leroy Paige was born in Mobile somewhere around the turn of the century, the son of a slave woman. When he was very young, he saw a baseball game. What really fascinated Leroy was the man on the mound. Watching his movements closely, Leroy began pitching rocks off the sandlot in imitation of the man he had seen in the pitcher's box.

By the time he was twelve, Leroy was pitching real live baseballs; and pitching against grown men. At seventeen he was already a legend on the sandlots. He could strike out any man that swung a bat. Then he got a job with a semi-pro team and was billed as the "strike-out king from Mobile." For the next quarter-century, Leroy Paige was striking out batters from the Panhandle to the Atlantic Coast. The legend grew and grew and Leroy acquired the nickname by which he forever after would be known. "Satchel" they called him, Satchel Paige, because of the little satchel he carried with him from sandlot to sandlot.

During the 1930's, Satchel was known as "The World's Greatest Pitcher, guaranteed to strike out the first nine batters." Fans came from miles around to see him pitch. He was like a freak in a circus sideshow, a wonder of nature. Satchel pitched his best games during these years but the color barrier kept him out of the majors. He was well known to baseball people everywhere, though. Dizzy Dean and Bob Feller called him "the greatest pitcher who ever lived." Abe Saperstein, manager of the Harlem Globetrotters, thought so, too, and so did Bill Veeck. But their hands were tied until Jackie Robinson broke the color barrier after World War II.

By then it was 1948 and Satchel Paige was in his 43rd year . . . some say 49th. The Cleveland Indians were gunning for the pennant that year and they desperately needed an extra pitcher. Could the great Satchel help them this late in his career? Afraid to chance the pennant on an old man, the Indians kept him in reserve until they ran out of pitchers. Then, in a crucial game, "Ol' Satch" was called out to face the great Joe DiMaggio before a packed house in Yankee Stadium. Satchel quickly made DiMaggio a believer by striking him out with the bases loaded and the Indians went on to win the World Championship. Satchel won six games that year and lost only one, on a fluke play. The next year he was back again, then went on to St. Louis and pitched several years for the Browns.

In 1965, Satchel returned to Mobile and helped christen the new auditorium by appearing with the Harlem Globetrotters. All this time Satchel Paige has never given up pitching. In his sixties, he claims that his arm is as good as ever. "All I have to do to get wound up," he says, "is to shake hands with the catcher." Bill Veeck yet maintains that for one inning he is still the best pitcher in baseball. Two years ago, Satch was still pitching for the Kansas City Athletics.

Satchel Paige might have as good a reason as any man to be bitter. But he isn't. He knows he was the greatest pitcher who ever lived and so do his fans who used to watch him stride up to the mound back in the thirties and deliver a fast ball that would knock your eyeballs out.

Mobile's Negroes were always a notch above the rest of the colored brethren in other towns throughout the South, even back in slave days. The Negroes in Mobile didn't usually pick cotton or hoe weeds way out in the fields somewhere. They stayed close to home, were personal servants, ran errands, helped their masters in business. As a result they learned to read and write and to compete in the free world when emancipation came. As a matter of fact, many of them were free already and some even owned slaves, themselves.

No one was surprised when the first Negro doctor set up practice in Mobile. Dr. R. A. Boyd treated patients along Davis Avenue for quite a few years. Besides being a top notch doctor, he had the distinction of being the first Negro ever to graduate from Harvard Medical School.

A few years later, Dr. George H. Wilkerson succeeded Dr. Boyd as Davis Avenue's top doctor, until Dr. Franklin inherited the title.

Besides the medical profession, Mobile has always had a flock of outstanding preachers of the gospel. A. J. Warner was pastor of the Big Zion Church. Pastor Warner supplemented his preaching activities by running for sheriff of Mobile County and for other state offices.

V. K. Glanton was for many years, pastor of the Stone Street Baptist Church, Mobile's oldest colored church.

Then there was the good Reverend A. F. Owens. Way back around the first World War, Reverend Owens started a very charitable project which has continued to this very day. Every Thanksgiving he would round up all the turkeys he could beg, borrow or buy. Then he would fix up complete Thanksgiving lunches and take them to the county jail. Even the hardened birds behind the bars were touched by the old Negro minister's thoughtfulness.

Of the many remarkable personalities on Davis Avenue, none has a success story quite like the Rt. Reverend, Bishop William Thomas Phillips, founder and pastor of the Adams Street Apostolic Overcoming Holiness Church of God, Inc. Bishop Phillips came to Mobile in 1916 for a ten-day visit. He looked around, felt a spiritual vacuum and set about the task of blowing into it the breath of life. Up until then the Bishop had been a roving evangelist, but now in Mobile, he organized his own church. Three years later, he saw the wisdom of incorporating. It was then that the Lord must have decided to really bless the Bishop's work—the church began to grow and grow.

"Ask and it shall be given you," was one of the Bishop's favorite scriptures. He "asked" by passing the hat and the blessings began to flow. Soon, there was need for missions, then more missions and the field broadened and the harvest ripened. The Church bought a publishing house valued at $50,000; then a Saints Rescue Home for $75,000; then increased the value of the Adams Street Complex to $150,000. Nine hundred missionaries were then sent out to organize churches in every state of the union, to Africa, India and the West Indies.

Bishop Phillips' work did not elude the eyes of his fellow Mobilians nor his fellow Alabamians. A Mobile group honored him with "Bishop Phillips Day" a few years ago, and several colleges pinned on him the titles of Bachelor of Theology, Doctor of Divinity and Doctor of Laws.

The Bishop could have retired a long time ago. He had already accomplished as much as any man had a right to expect. But the idea of retirement is a repugnant notion to the dynamic Bishop. As long as there was a soul to save and a hat to pass, the Bishop would be about his Master's work. He only recently purchased another publishing house for $275,000. In 1968 he bought out the Toulminville Baptist Church, one of the largest white Baptist churches on the Gulf Coast, for well in excess of a quarter-million dollars.

Bishop Phillips has never believed in standing still and he still doesn't. If he lives long enough, he may very well establish the first mission on the moon for stranded space travelers who look as though they might want to join up with the Apostolic Overcoming Holiness Church of God, Inc.

Chapter 25

Everything's Made for Love . . . and Money

Frank Boykin jumped on his horse and dashed after the North-bound train. The passengers looked out the windows, then withdrew in terror. Who was this bandit so bold as to be chasing a train in the broad open daylight they thought. The horseman was too far away to be seen distinctly but he was clearly gaining on his prey with each turn of the wheel. After miles of hot pursuit the man on horseback overtook the passenger train as it was pulling up a long hill. With amazing agility, he leaped onto the coach and the riders braced themselves.

There was money on that train and the horseman knew it, ever since he learned it was leaving Mobile. But Frank Boykin wasn't interested in money that day. He walked down the aisle until he found a pretty girl looking up at him in wide-eyed amazement. Miss Ocllo Gunn really wasn't surprised at anything Frank Boykin would do. But when he fell at her feet and proposed in full view of a train full of passengers, she was so shocked that she accepted. With the biggest of his deals closed, young Frank Boykin let out a whoop, jumped back on his trusty steed and galloped back to his lumbercamp, shouting, "Everything's made for love!"

Frank Boykin was still a young man when he married his beloved Ocllo, young and on top of the world. But his fortunes hadn't always been so high. At the age of eight, he went to work on the Alabama, Tennessee and Northern Railroad, hauling water to construction workers at 35¢ a day. Even then he was approaching his task with characteristic zeal. When the foreman asked him to find another boy who would work for 35¢ a day, Frank rigged up a makeshift shoulder yoke so that he could carry two buckets a trip and earn 70¢ a day. A few years later, he quit school altogether because "my family was so poor, we would have got the prize if there'd a been any."

By the time he was twelve, Frank had thought of so many ways to be of service to the railroad that he was given the highfaluting title of "Chief Dispatcher and Conductor." In no time at all, he knew every person within miles of the railroad and was making so many suggestions that, at 14, he became a roving agent and intelligence assistant to John T. Cochran, president of the railroad line. Then he was put in charge of the commissary on the train and made a big success of that sideline enterprise by promoting it up and down the line from Mobile to Choctaw County.

As Frank Boykin rode the train back and forth through the back woods, his eyes began to settle on the beautiful forests that stretched before him. "Someday, I'll own some of that land," he thought to himself. But "someday" came sooner than he thought. Learning that whole acres of Washington County land could be purchased for a pocket full of change, he began buying up some of that land. Then he learned that it could be leased for even less. Setting up a little saw mill, he leased a couple hundred acres and got a sizable contract from Southern Railroad. Over the next few decades, his contracts increased so fast he began buying land outright, then selling part of it at a good price and buying more land with the profit. When the paper mill boom hit Mobile, Frank Boykin had one of his fortunes made. He didn't stop there, though. Besides his real estate speculating and his saw mills, Boykin made a few smaller fortunes in the turpentine and pine resin business. Eventually, he became the wealthiest man in Mobile with a 17,000 acre game reserve besides 150,000 acres in Washington and Mobile Counties.

With his many fortunes made, Boykin turned to another field for which he was ideally suited—politics. With his love for people, his knack for remembering names and his abundant energy, the genial Boykin rolled to victory in 1935 in the special election for Congress. He had conquered Mobile, now he set his sights on Washington. The capital was a little bigger city than Mobile, but Frank Boykin, with his loud, booming voice, soon made himself heard by the Roosevelt Administration. FDR was not so popular in Alabama and Boykin aroused the ire of some of his constituents by sending the President generous supplies of venison from his hunting grounds in Washington County. But Alabama needed the President's support and Frank Boykin knew how to rub people the right way.

One of the projects that Boykin was interested in was the building of a system of transportation across the Mobile Delta. He gave the project his full support and sat back to watch what happened. Way back in 1927,

Boykin's old boss, John T. Cochran, had been instrumental in getting a bridge and system of causeways built across Mobile Bay linking Mobile with Baldwin County. But the Cochran Bridge was soon outdated. When in 1937, John E. Toomey, director of the First National Bank, made the tunnel proposal, Boykin's administration courting began to pay off. Wayne F. Palmer's financial plan to raise four million dollars was backed by the Public Works Administration and the work was soon underway to build a time and distance-saving tunnel under the Mobile River. The tunnel was built on dry land, miraculously floated into place and by February 20, 1941, a new type of subaqueous tunnel was completed and ready for operation.

It was a cold, drizzling day when the tunnel opened up for business. But it didn't stifle the enthusiasm of curious Mobilians who had been watching the construction work for three years. On that long awaited day, several thousand people gathered at the Government Street entrance. When Mayor Cecil T. Bates gave the signal, the crowd began to move forward and briskly walked under the Mobile River in twelve minutes. A Great Dane named "Poochy" made the historic trip, along with a woman pushing her infant child and a little girl on roller skates. At ten o'clock, the pedestrians were cleared out of the way and a stream of auto traffic began to flow that has never stopped. The tunnel had been named for Alabama's famed Congressman John Hollis Bankhead, Sr., once Speaker of the House. Bankhead never lived to see the tunnel but several years later Frank Boykin brought down his grandaughter, Tallulah Bankhead, to appear in a play at the Murphy High School Auditorium. After the play, Tallulah got into a cab and drove through the tunnel named for her grandfather, waving a Confederate flag all the way.

The Bankhead Tunnel wasn't the only big project Frank Boykin watched come to Mobile. As Mobile's Congressman, he helped to promote Brookley Field, a gigantic Air Force Base that was to become the biggest thing that ever hit the port city. Mobile already had a small, commercial airport that eventually was to be known as Bates Field. In 1940, the War Department moved the commercial airport out and began construction of the new facility to be named for Captain Wendell H. Brookley who had been killed in the crash of a military plane at Bolling Field, Washington, D.C. in 1934. When Pearl Harbor was bombed, Brookley Field began to bulge. By the end of the war nearly twelve thousand employees were on the Brookley payroll. Mobile's population swelled. When the war ended Brookley continued to grow. By the time Defense Secretary Robert McNamara announced in 1964 that Brookley would be gradually "phased out," the Air Force Base was providing bread and butter for 15,000 Mobilians and their families.

Frank Boykin was elated to see Brookley coming and sorry to see it go, but he was too busy to worry too much about either. On Capitol Hill he had become much the topic of conversation. With his cheery "Howdy Partner" greeting and his colorful quips, he was a natural for reporters. Once he was asked his opinion of a loan the United States had just made to Pakistan.

"I don't even know where Pakistan is," replied Frank, "but they must be awful good folks if we gave 'em that much money."

Speaking to a group of Yankees, Boykin warned, "You'd better come down to Mobile while you're still alive. That's the closest to heaven some of you'll ever get." Then he would go on to extol the port city. "How can we miss," he would say, "when we've got the best water, the best transportation, the best land and the best people in the whole world?"

When not praising his hometown, Boykin was busy promoting legislation and making money. Among the grandiose schemes he tried to push through Congress was a canal across Mexico and the Tennessee-Tombigbee Waterway which would provide a channel all the way to Sioux City, Iowa. The Mexican canal still seems a long way off but the Tennessee-Tombigbee is an idea that is beginning to excite Mobilians more each year. Boykin also tried to promote a commemorative postage stamp for Mobile but the Post Office wouldn't go along with it. Another one of his projects was a four-lane Mobile-to-Prichard highway.

In support of all his projects Boykin approached the tasks in his characteristically flamboyant style. Frank called his style "promoting," while some Washingtonians called it "lobbying." Drew Pearson, who never did quite understand Frank, described his promotions as "amazingly flagrant." Drew Pearson was more than amazed when once Boykin decided that he needed Congressional support on a bill that would aid the paper mill industry. Boykin had gotten his inspiration when Congressman Howard Smith of Virginia made an unflattering remark about racoons. "Why, coon meat is the greatest," claimed Frank. Then he set up a special dinner and invited members of the Fish and Wildlife Committee to come see for themselves how coon meat tastes. When the commitee members arrived for the dinner they found that an auxilliary purpose of the dinner was to discuss legislation. Then Frank innocently suggested that they adjourn to the dining room of the Speaker of the House, where Frank went about convincing the committee members how they should vote. Genial Frank forgot to tell the committee how much stock he owned in the paper mills.

He was absent-minded sometimes, but he had a way with people. Besides, what was good for Frank Boykin was good for Mobile.

Drew Pearson got him into hot water on that one. But Frank Boykin was used to trouble. It seemed to follow him around wherever he went and he usually stumbled right into its path. Almost always, Boykin's troubles had humorous overtones. Like the time one of his employees at his deer range shot a bear that was making off with all the honey. Frank got the bear meat and generously donated it to a Mobile hospital. Then a game warden came along and the case went to court. Before the judge could make up his mind that the Alabama ban on bear-hunting had been violated, Frank had half of south Alabama arguing over the best way to cook bear meat. The judge finally threw up his hands and tossed everybody concerned out of court.

Most of Frank's troubles were funny but one case was a little less amusing. A tax fraud case had involved two prominent Mobilians who went crying to Frank to do something about it. All Frank did was to call on a friend in Washington and tell him to "give 'em the works if they're guilty but if they're not, quit worryin' 'em to death." For such a simple act of kindness Frank heard loud charges of "influence peddling." When the Maryland land cases came up, Frank was convicted and fined forty thousand dollars after star witness Bobby Kennedy finished his testimony. The money meant very little to Frank but he was very hurt to think that some people might misunderstand. A few years later, though, on a cold December day, Frank picked up the morning paper to find that President Lyndon Johnson had pardoned him. "It's a fine Christmas present," is all Frank would say but his spirits were considerably uplifted and he went out and made another million dollars.

Making a million dollars is easy as falling off a log for Frank, though. A short time ago, he showed a few skeptical people just how easy it was. He obtained an option to buy several thousand acres of timber in Mississippi for eleven million dollars. Then he picked up the phone and found someone who would buy the land for twelve million. With a minimum of effort and very little haggling, he had made a cool million dollars.

Frank Boykin was finally beaten in the "9-8" Congressional race of 1962. After a quarter of a century in Congress, he went out the same way he got in—by accident, in a special election. This didn't slow him down much, though. It only gave him more time to enjoy his friends, his deer hunts, his dogs and his money. He rented a suite in the Admiral Semmes Hotel and went right to work promoting his business interests and the city of Mobile. Mobile responded by having a Frank Boykin Day and George Wallace made him a special emissary to Washington.

Time may go flying by but it'll have to hurry to catch up with Frank Boykin. At 83, he's still fighting old age as if he's going to beat it. In his ever-loving way, he goes rolling along, slapping backs, blowing kisses and making money with the same zest he applied in making his first million and in winning the hand of Ocllo Gunn.

Chapter 26

Battleship Pete and the Boys

Peter Bernard was a drifter. He was born in Wisconsin but he got the wanderlust soon after he was married. After all, he had to make a living and what he knew best, there just wasn't much demand for in Wisconsin. Not many ships were being built that far inland.

So Peter took off on a jaunt around the country. He went to New Jersey and rocked up and down the Atlantic Seaboard. Then one day in 1910, he came to Mobile and got himself a job in the shipyard. He made pretty good money in the shipyard and sent a good portion of it back to his family in Wisconsin. A couple of years later, he made it back home but the family was gone and left no forwarding address.

Crestfallen, Peter took stock of his assets. He had little in the way of money. About the only thing he had acquired was the imposing nickname of "Battleship Pete." Returning to Mobile, Battleship Pete went back to build-

ing ships. World War I was in its peak year and the bat-
tleships had a place for Pete. With no family to support,
Pete accumulated a little capital, as time went by. When
he retired from the shipyard, he opened up a little tavern
near the waterfront which he called "The Oyster Bar."

One could find most of the town characters hanging around "The Oyster Bar" at any given time. As often
as not, they would be in the middle of a hot poker game.
One day, the poker game was moved across the street to
the CIO Hall. It was good luck for Pete. A photographer
took a photo and sent it off to *The Shipbuilder* magazine. The poker photo came off the press captioned with
Peter Bernard's name.

Up in Detroit, Peter Bernard, Jr., a successful realtor,
had been searching for his father for forty years. Until
he saw the picture, he had given up hope of ever finding
anything but his grave. Now, here was a Peter Bernard
still living. Could it possibly be the same one? Peter Bernard, Jr. called Mobile, decided Ol' Pete was his long,
lost father, then grabbed a plane and "The Oyster Bar"
witnessed a tearful reunion. Two years later, his eighty-
seven-year-old sister hopped a bus from California and
made her way to "The Oyster Bar" to see Ol' Pete.

Battleship Pete was in his eighties when his second
wife died. Inconsolable, he sold the tavern and bought
an island out in Mobile Bay. Little Sand Island was its
real name until Battleship Pete's invasion. He called it
Goat Island and his friends gave him a new tag—the
Hermit of Goat Island. To the island, Pete brought all
his worldly possessions; his furniture, his personal ef-
fects, his juke box. Right in the middle of the little shack
he had built, he placed his treasured juke box. It wouldn't
play, of course, but it reminded him of the old days
back in "The Oyster Bar" when there was always a poker
game or a song going on.

Pete made infrequent trips into town. Once a month, he would get into his little motor boat and chug into town to pick up his social security check and to buy a few groceries. His life was lonely but not uneventful. Once a hurricane blew his boat out into the bay and he was marooned until rescued by the Coast Guard. Then his outboard motor played out and he was cast adrift on the bay. This time it was the Brookley Air Force that came to the rescue.

It was after this that his old friends decided that Pete needed a new boat and a new motor. The boat was filled with holes, barely rising above the water line. In a touching ceremony down at the waterfront, Battleship Pete was presented with a brand new boat and outboard motor. As soon as he had brushed away the tears, he jumped in the boat and went chugging back out to his Goat Island haven. He came into town a little more often after that. Once, the wrath of Mobile was heaped upon a heartless thief who snitched Pete's boat and motor while the old man, then in his 94th year, had gone to pick up his check.

On the third day in April, 1966, Battleship Pete left his beloved Goat Island for the last time. He had enjoyed a serene life on the Island all these years, away from the hurly-burly of civilization, away from the speed and racket of men and machines. He had only been in town a brief time when the very thing he had sought to avoid, a honking, speeding machine driven by a man in a hurry gunned him down and killed him at the age of 96.

Battleship Pete had been one of many characters who covered the Mobile waterfront. Many of them were Pete's old cronies who often visited his Oyster Bar. One such man was Mose Bernstein. "The Umbrella Man," they called Mose, because of his peculiar habit of carrying a black umbrella everywhere he went, rain or shine.

When someone asked, "Why do you carry that umbrella?" Mose would only smile and say, "Because it can't walk."

Folks that knew him said Mose never forgot a name or a face. If true, it was because that was his business. For 53 years, Mose served the people of Mobile County as deputy sheriff. Once, he was standing around the courtroom when he thought he saw a familiar witness on the stand. Mose called him down and the records showed that the strange witness was actually wanted on a murder charge and hadn't been seen in Mobile in ten years. The witness was promptly re-incarcerated.

As a younger man, Mose used to ride around Mobile on horseback, serving papers. Once he raided a dice game in Plateau and piled 22 prisoners on a springboard wagon. On the way back to the Mobile jail, he saw two escaped convicts jumping from a train. He stopped his wagon, chased down the convicts, handcuffed them together and piled them on the jail-bound wagon.

Mose did all of his amazing work despite the fact that he was only five feet-two inches tall, had never learned to drive a car and never carried a gun. In 1913 he was praised by Woodrow Wilson when he helped protect that President while he was in Mobile. Lyndon Johnson sent him a note fifty years later, congratulating him on a job well done. The President's note came while Mose was being recognized as the oldest law enforcement officer in the nation. It was a citation well deserved. Mose Bernstein was active as bailiff only hours before his death at the age of ninety.

One of the Umbrella Man's colleagues was Jeremiah "Gummy" Flournoy, the newspaper man who chewed gum so rapidly you could hardly understand him talk. And you had to understand him talk, that is, if you worked for the Mobile Register. "Gummy," it seems, was a newswriter who didn't write. He was of the old school, one of those who had a nose for the news, who was always at the scene when the event was taking place. Then when the incident transpired, he simply picked up the nearest telephone and dictated the story over the wire.

Sometimes, "Gummy" got to chewing and talking so fast that he thought himself ahead of the actual events. Most of the time, this anticipatory sense made him look like a brilliant reporter. But even the best get caught, sometimes. In a moonshine case presided over by Judge Tisdale Touart, "Gummy" sensed a quick conviction for the moonshiners. He quickly phoned in a "conviction" and the story broke. In this instance, however, Judge Touart decided to insist on a chemical analysis of the jug contents. The arresting officer couldn't produce any evidence from the jug so the man was acquitted. "Gummy" was cited for contempt.

Both "Gummy" and Mose Bernstein kept a sharp eye on Roy Dickerson, the ex-bankrobber and escape-artist. Dickerson robbed the bank in Phenix City, Alabama, of $14,000 in 1920 and was sent to Kilby. But Kilby couldn't hold him. He escaped several times before the Governor finally paroled him to Mobile. In the port city, Dickerson became such a model citizen that "Big Jim" Folsom gave him a state job and appointed him honorary colonel on the Governor's staff.

Sam Zemurray came to Mobile as a kid from Russia. "Banana King Sam," folks called him, as he peddled bananas on the streets. One day, he bought half-a-boatload of ripe bananas and jumped on the train to Selma where he figured to get higher prices for the bananas. By the time he got to Prichard, the bananas were getting sort of sickly-looking so Sam sent a batch of telegrams to stations along the track. When he got to Selma, "Banana

King Sam" had made a fruitful gain. Eventually, he made a sizable profit, then bought a plantation in Honduras. When revolution broke out, Sam rescued the President of Honduras in a boat, then took him to New Orleans. When the plans were set, he sailed El Presidente back to Honduras and with an army of 600 men seized control of the government. Sam's plantation thrived after that and the Banana King went on to become the multi-millionaire president of United Fruit.

Then there was and is the arresting Richard A. Tullis who proudly refers to himself as "The Windbag." Mr. Tullis has come to be almost a landmark around Mobile. Even today, at 82, he can be seen ambling down the avenues, sporting a ring on every finger, with dozens of stickpins on his chest and, likely as not, followed by a pack of dogs. He can tell you all about his adventurous life, his four ex-wives, and the hundreds of office buildings he owns. The most arresting thing about Mr. Tullis is his face, the lean, lined, bearded face of a saint or sage. He was recently "discovered" by the artist William Nolen-Schmidt and today the venerable Mr. Tullis does as much sitting as he does walking.

Caldwell Delaney, the decorous director of the City Museum, tells about the time he was talking to author William March when a neighborhood school let out for the day. As the young children filed past them, Delaney remarked how sweet and delicate the little kiddies looked. Whereupon March snorted and began to expound on the quantity of malicious intent lurking in the minds of little children. March, at the time Vice-President of the Waterman Steamship Company, went on from that poignant observation to write *The Bad Seed,* a Broadway hit which caused one critic to hail him as "the great unrecognized genius of our time."

Another author who has managed to stir up a lot of conversation is the poet-painter-sculptor-folklorist, Julian Lee Rayford. "Judy," as his friends call him, has just about done it all. Working as an artist for the W.P.A. back in the thirties, he was one who didn't piddle around. As a folk singer in New York City and a sculptor in Latin America, Judy was widely acclaimed. His biggest claim to fame, however, is his work as a folklorist. Besides raising Joe Cain, Judy wrote a book on folklore which he called *Whistlin' Woman and Crowin' Hen,* one of the works which prompted an encyclopedia editor to dub him "one of the four living authorities on the restoration of the folk story to its original source."

In 1964 Judy was commissioned by the city to do a simple little plaque to be presented at the dedication of the Phoenix Fire Museum. It only cost $150 and was to have inscribed the name of the Mayor, Joseph N. Langan. Before the ceremony took place, Lady Bird Johnson announced she would be passing through Mobile about that time. So naturally the First Lady was invited to say a few words and to make the presentation of the plaque. The date was merely set up from September 29 to October 9; all well and good. Except that on October 1, Mobile had a new Mayor coming into office. Mayor Charles Trimmier, slightly upset to find that his name was not on the plaque, ordered a new one—this time the plaque would cost one full grand. So "Judy" set to work on another more elaborate one, which he barely finished by the time the Lady Bird flew into town.

Many Mobilians still remember the time another Mobile Mayor, Harry T. Hartwell, welcomed Calvin Coolidge to the port city, claiming that "sunshine and flowers awaited his arrival." When Coolidge finally arrived in Mobile, it was in the dead of winter and the temperature was barely hovering above zero. Nevertheless, Mayor

Harry pranced down to the train station, outfitted in a white Irish linen suit. Coolidge stepped off the train without saying a word, then reached in his pocket, pulled out Harry's letter, reread it, then came out with a characteristic remark. "Kinda cool now, though," he said, then stuffed the letter back in his pocket.

Another high-spirited character was the Reverend Lester Spencer, Pastor of St. Mark's Methodist Church. Most Mobilians remember the time he rode a horse all the way to Baltimore to celebrate Methodism's 200th birthday in America. He returned to the pulpit none the worse for his strenuous effort except that his congregation noticed him saying "giddyup" when he should have been saying "Amen."

There were other notable personages, too. François Ludgére Diard, descendent of Fifise Langlois, took seriously his hobby of collecting historical relics. Besides autographs of Washington and Lincoln, he reputedly owned the wedding band of Charles LeMoyne and Catherine Thierry, parents of Bienville. When he died, Frank's collection of Mobiliana had the whole city agog.

Then there is Mike Blake, a modern woodsman to rival Sam Dale. Mike spent forty years looking for the ancient battlefield of Mobila and is still at it today, gleefully walking old Indian paths with the gusto of an adolescent.

J. Oliver Wintzell is a man that knows his oysters. Moving up to Mobile from Bayou La Batre, he went to Spring Hill College until he found out they didn't offer a degree in oysterneering. So he quit the college and opened up an Oyster House on Dauphin Street that has gained national prominence for the delicacy of its oysters and the writing on its walls. He still spends as much time around the Oyster Bar as he ever did, talking politics, greeting guests, chainsmoking cigars and generally keeping the air stirred up. His son, J.O. "Sonny" Wintzell keeps things stirred up, too. He recently stirred up the biggest argument to hit Mobile since the roaring twenties, a controversy that may not be settled for years to come. In the courts, on the land and under the sea the word that electrified Mobilians in 1967 was the same as that which petrified Mobilians of a century ago—Tecumseh.

Chapter 27

The Tecumseh Rises Again!

Hatchett Chandler, the Fort Morgan Curator, used to stand on the walls of the old fort and point out where the *Tecumseh* went down. If Hatchett knew where it was in 1966, he knew more than the United States Government. Years before the U.S. Coast and Geodetic Survey published a map which pinpointed exactly where the *Tecumseh* had sunk. Yet when the Smithsonian Institution sent its divers down in the winter of 1967, down to the exact point shown on the survey map, the divers came up with nothing but a mouthful of water. "Where was the *Tecumseh*?" the Smithsonian salvagers were asking. "Now who made off with the *Tecumseh*?"

Back at the Oyster Bar, Sonny Wintzell was chuckling to himself. He knew where the *Tecumseh* was, if nobody else did. After all, he hadn't spent $15,000 and ten years research into the matter for nothing. No, indeed. He knew, for example, that Farragut's flagship, a

giant, iron sea monster 225 feet long and 48 feet wide
had come barreling past Fort Morgan, had veered away
from the *Tennessee* and into the path of the mines. He
knew that the *Tecumseh* had gone down fast, perhaps
aided by Morgan's guns, had rolled over and been buried
for years in mud upside down, hidden to all but the most
scrutinizing divers. He knew all of this but he wasn't telling the Smithsonian people. Several years before he had
located the *Tecumseh*, himself, and had obtained some
salvage rights to the sunken vessel. After all, why not?
Sonny Wintzell was interested in commercial ventures
and, being a history buff, this seemed the perfect opportunity to combine business with pleasure. Besides,
nobody else had ever been interested in raising the
Tecumseh before. For a hundred years it had lain peacefully on the bottom of Mobile Bay, out of sight, out of
mind. Why, all of a sudden, had Smithsonian become
interested?

It was a question that intrigued not only Sonny Wintzell but all of Mobile. Who were these Yankee scavengers
returning to the scene of their crime? What Alabama had
sunk, had not Alabama a right to keep? And besides,
who owned the bottom of Mobile Bay?

When Smithsonian sent down its men and began to
seriously make plans for the salvaging of the *Tecumseh*,
Mobile began to murmur. When Smithsonian announced
that its intention was to resurrect the *Tecumseh* and
take it back to Washington, indignant protests were
lodged by Mobilians. "The *Tecumseh*," announced the
Smithsonian, "is the only salvagable example of the
monitor class of fighting ships that ushered in the era
of armored naval warfare. We mean to resurrect it for
our maritime museum."

Still, the *Tecumseh* had not been found and Sonny

Wintzell was not alarmed. If Smithsonian stuck to the Geodetic Survey, they never would find the sunken ship. Then, on February 1, 1967, the Smithsonian boys got off the beaten track. They stumbled onto a carcass sticking a bare seven feet out of the mud, covered with silt. The Feds were jubilant. The announcement of the discovery made headlines from coast to coast and Smithsonian began to make more definite plans for salvage operations. Dr. Alan H. Rosenstein of the Marine Engineering Laboratory, Captain Willard F. Searle, Navy Supervisor of Salvage, and Col. John McGruder began to make all sorts of tests. Their reports were unanimously encouraging. The *Tecumseh* was in almost a perfect state of preservation. And the bodies—maybe they would be mummified. There were 93 men who went down with the ship, 93 men who possibly could still be sitting there with eyes open to greet the first diver who broke into the cabins. Or maybe the salt water had overflowed into the cabins. Then there would be nothing but the bare skeletal remains of Captain Craven and his boys.

"But now just a durn minute," piped Sonny Wintzell. "That's all fine and dandy but I've got the salvage rights."

To prove it, Sonny hired the brilliant young attorney M. A. "Bubba" Marsal, and sought to enjoin the Smithsonian Institution from meddling with his ship. George Wallace, he claimed, had told him to go ahead and "get 'er up." And who the hell was the Federal Government to be bucking George Wallace?

The case was set to be heard in circuit court in March, that is, until the U.S. Attorney moved to transfer the case to Federal Court. After being kicked around from court to court, the trial was finally set for the first week in May—Sonny Wintzell versus the Smithsonian Institution. Meanwhile, Sonny went back to eating oysters as a few more actors walked on stage.

The Alabama Department of Conservation claimed possession of the *Tecumseh* because "it is in Alabama mud." The director, Claude Kelly, said he wasn't giving title to anyone.

Then State Representative Robert S. Edington got a resolution passed in the Legislature, creating a committee to investigate the possibility of the State of Alabama raising the *Tecumseh*. After all, hadn't the State been able to raise enough funds to get the *U.S.S. Alabama* to Mobile? Why couldn't the State raise the *Tecumseh*?

Then the Mobile Junior Chamber of Commerce got into the act. This, indeed, was a force to be reckoned with. The Mobile Jaycees, the most energetic and outstanding organization in the State year-in and year-out, the Mobile Jaycees who had already been responsible for such productions as *The Azalea Trail* and *America's Junior Miss Pageant;* now they were striking up the war drums.

"We are prepared," said Jaycee President Fred Killion, "to undertake the salvage, restoration, preservation and public display of the *Tecumseh*. We are opposed to any effort to remove the vessel from the boundaries of the State of Alabama."

In the face of this wave of opposition the Smithsonian faltered just a bit. They had encountered opposition before in their numerous projects but never such an outcry like this. Then in May the trial came up in Federal District Court. Wintzell produced his evidence and arguments and the United States moved for dismissal of suit. After a week in court, U.S. Judge Daniel Thomas dismissed the case but gave Wintzell a chance to amend his pleadings. The case was reset for August 2, but Wintzell did not respond and the Judge again dismissed the case. Apparently this ended the controversy. But only apparently. New battles began to be waged, diplomatic battles. "What we must do," Robert Edington was saying, "is to persuade the Smithsonian it is in the best interest of maritime history to leave the *Tecumseh* in the area where it became famous."

Meanwhile, the Smithsonian was making big plans. The whole operation would cost in the neighborhood of three million dollars; it would take two years to complete and would be somewhat hazardous due to the tons of live ammunition and loaded guns on board the ship. The Government appointed a special commission to take care of the bodies—they would be buried en masse in Washington's National Cemetery. Then the divers went down and brought up the *Tecumseh*'s anchor and put it on display. "Look for the *Tecumseh* to break water in 1970," the Smithsonian said in the summer of 1968, confident now that they would be the ones to do the job. After the long fight, the case of the *Tecumseh* seemed to be cut and dried.

But J. O. "Sonny" Wintzell has not yet abandoned ship. He has hired two more lawyers to aid Marsal and a local researcher named Leon Raley who has spent a decade of study on the *Tecumseh* and who has reached some strange conclusions. "I can raise 'er in ninety days," maintains Wintzell. "And at half the cost. Why don't they give me a shot at 'er, then settle the ownership question after I've saved tax money?"

According to Wintzell, the battle is not yet over and from all appearances, it seems that the *Tecumseh* has a long way to go to get to the Washington museum. Meanwhile, Sonny keeps eating oysters and the Smithsonian keeps on diving, maintaining a sharp lookout for trespassers, explosives and sharks of all sorts.

During the *Tecumseh* controversy, Hatchett Chandler was one of the more outraged Mobilians. He wanted the *Tecumseh* to sit right in the middle of the Fort Morgan Museum. The battle should have come a few years earlier—Hatchett would have been right in the middle of it, then, with both feet kicking. For he was a man who loved controversy. Hatchett died a few days after the dismissal of the last *Tecumseh* suit. At 87, he was too weak to breathe much fire at the Federal invaders. He would be happy to know, though, that he, himself, went out with a bang.

Long before he died, Hatchett had picked out his own burial site. He wanted to lie near his beloved Fort Morgan —about ninety feet from the wall, to be exact. He had gone so far as to obtain permission and to announce to the public his chosen site of interment. And when he died in August of 1967, it was taken for granted that his remains would be properly carried under. Then the fatal day came—the newspapers announced his death, saying that funeral services would be conducted on the following Sunday. Reverend Howard Welch, Pastor of the Foley Lutheran Church, presided over the funeral services that afternoon and about 4:30 Higgins-Brown Mortuary brought up the body for burial. Bay Minette Attorney Kenneth Cooper delivered a eulogy, then the casket men looked around for a hole.

But there was no hole. Not only that, Roger C. Kirkland, Secretary of the Fort Morgan Historical Commission, served a resolution to Foley Attorney Forrest Griffin which stated that Hatchett could not be buried at Fort Morgan—he must be buried at a little spot back in the woods called "The Lost Cemetery."

Hatchett's friend brought him back to Foley but the fat was in the fire. Several members of the burying party appealed to Governor Lurleen Wallace. "So what," they said, "if Hatchett had become irascible in his old age, so what if he referred in print to State Conservation members as 'Holy Apes.' Hadn't he come to Fort Morgan years before when it was nothing but a sand dune grown up in weeds? Hadn't he lived out his adult years at Fort Morgan sleeping with the gnats and pawing off mosquitoes, enduring the bitter cold and scorching heat? Was a little plot of sand too much to ask for years of devotion?"

The Alabama House of Representatives passed a quick resolution asking for permission to bury Hatchett at Fort Morgan. The resolution was tabled in the Senate but it didn't matter very much. Public opinion seemed to be clearly on the side of Hatchett Chandler. Sensing their advantage, Hatchett's friends brought him back to his chosen burial site. This time, they meant business— State Police or no State Police. Several hundred people joined in the ceremonies—one man toted a shotgun; another had a pistol bulging out his pocket; children pitched in and helped dig the grave. Some had spoons, some pawed at the ground with their hands while adults manned the spades. Then the second rites were held and while a young boy stood and played taps, the worn and weary body of Hatchett Chandler was lowered into the grave, one full week after he had died. It had been a good fight but Hatchett Chandler, in death as in life, finally got his way.

Chapter 28

A Revolution In Mobile

Government Street was once far and away the most beautiful stretch of road in America, two miles of ante-bellum styled homes graced with an embellishment of roses, azaleas and oaks. Today, it is still attractive but more like a slowly aging belle fighting against grey hair, fillings and wrinkles.

How Government Street declined is an old and simple story, a story that is being retold and relived in practically every southern city—a widow dies, the heirs are gone or broke, they sell to a chain store, a real estate company or an oil company. The home is demolished, the trees are cut and the rubbage is carted away, replaced by a bright billboard, a cut-rate supermarket or a shiny new service station. "A sign of the times," the people say. "You can't stop progress. We're growing."

"Yes," the dissenters say, "we are growing. Like a cancer or a fungus. But we are growing."

In most southern cities, there are a number of genteel residents who refuse to equate progress with simple increase in construction. They like to think that there is something of value to the aestheic notion. But more often than not, they become discouraged by the dollar sign, turn aside and painfully watch their town's erosion. Mobile had its own group that could have suffered the same agonies. The Mobile Historic Preservation Society was organized in 1935. For years, members of the Society busied themselves collecting papers and historical relics, marking sites and generally promoting interest in the history of the area. They didn't engage in much controversy because there was none.

Then the vultures came. The first big bite they took came out of the Government Street hide. In time, the vultures would have devoured the whole body had not the Preservation Society, the Jaycees and a number of other local organizations taken the lead to stop the carnage. There were fights in court; the societies pressured the City Commission to pass ordinances restricting the destruction of property. "You will not wreck our city," the locals shouted at the intruders. "Mobile will never be a great city by virtue of size. We mean to see that it retains its reputation for scenic beauty and charm."

The societies meant it. But this negativism was only the beginning. Having struck in self defense, the local organizations took to the offensive. They persuaded the city to buy Oakleigh, where the Historic Preservation Society set up headquarters. Then they began to organize historical tours, while the Jaycees, of course, were promoting the Azalea Trail.

The result of all of this was that all Mobilians began to take a new pride in their community and to realize the potentialities of tourism—like the traditional Mobile

Belle—the more beautiful she is, the more attention she attracts. The spirit proved contagious. Mobilians began to look ahead in all directions. Mobile College was founded, then the University of South Alabama. In its own way, the city was undergoing a sort of renaissance.

The new spirit had its comic effect, too. In 1961, Mobile celebrated its 250th Anniversary and a rabid wave of civic pride broke loose—all the men in town grew beards, the ladies dressed up in the elaborate gowns of bygone years and giant picnics were held in Bienville Square. Strangers passing through town thought the community had gone mad. But it wasn't the first time outsiders thought Mobile had gone a little wacky. In 1959, the city's banning of spiked heels caused more national comment than any other legislation since Peter the Great told the eighteenth century Russians to shear their beards and trim their coattails.

It happened like this: On October 15th of that year, Commissioner Charles Hackmeyer came to the council meeting steaming mad. Another woman was suing the city, claiming she caught her heel in a drainage vent and twisted her ankle. "That makes fifty times we've been sued for that kinda rot," said Charley. "I move we do something about it."

So the City Council did something about it. They passed an ordinance banning the use of heels higher than an inch and a half and less than an inch in diameter. None of the Council was prepared for the frenzy that followed. When the news hit the wire services, Mobile was back in the nation's limelight. A New York manufacturer sent a carton of two dozen bottles of perfume—the brand name was "High Heel"—and a note enclosed that said, "Mobile ladies can wear this if nothing else." A Philadelphia inventor read of the incident and sent his latest device—an invention to save milady's heels and to insure safety. A young Shreveport girl wrote, "I hope Shreveport does the same thing before I break my fool neck just to be in style." And a soldier from Korea wrote, "Don't ban sweaters!" Mayor Joseph Langan was interviewed by a Hollywood radio station and the *Mobile Register* bemoaned the fact that "Mobile was getting national back-handed fame because of another funny law." Before it was over, Mobile's heels touched off a national debate on the wearing of high heels, the health, style, etc.

City Hall had about recovered from that episode when the pigeon controversy exploded. Ever since anybody could remember Mobile had pigeons all over the place. They walked all over town, usually minded their own business and never offended anybody. The worst thing they did, they did in public but that was no worse than what the local politicians did in private. Of course, they weren't the most sanitary birds in the world but probably nobody in Mobile ever got more than a slight case of diarrhea. Nobody was really much worried about pigeons until Ray Foster of Hammond, Louisiana walked into City Hall one day and started spouting off a list of diseases that would choke a commissioner. "Pigeons," he said, "are right at the bottom of parrot fever, cryptococcus meningitis, salmonella-typhimorium, areola burliatis and histoplasmosis."

Arthur Outlaw looked up at Foster in utter amazement. "You can't be serious?" he asked.

"Yep," said Foster. "Not only that but we strongly suspect these pigeons to be laden with kleptomaniatitus."

"Why, those nasty little devils," said Lambert Mims. Then the Commissioners sat back to think things over. Pigeons had been a little something of an issue for many years in Mobile but nobody ever did anything about it. The city code had an ordinance prohibiting pigeons from flying at large and there was once a $100 fine for letting private pigeons fly the coop. But to poison the pigeons en masse—this was something else. The Commission meditated long and hard until Arthur Outlaw hit on a brilliant line of logic.

"Well, it's already been publicized," he reasoned. "So we might as well go ahead and do it."

So Ray Foster and the All-State Pest Exterminating Company set to work. The pigeons began dropping like flies and City Hall was besieged with complaints of cruelty to birds. After a while the cries died down and the pigeons took the hint. But a few years later, they were back again and so were the pest control boys, seeking to make another fast buck. These days City Hall is avoiding the inflammatory issue of pigeons while a well known Mobilian is trying to come up with a birth control remedy for pigeons. "Un-sexticide" he calls it. Meanwhile, the pigeons still haunt Mobile.

Before the pigeon issue had settled down good, the dogs started acting up. On January 3, 1967, the Commission passed a dog law and the first month saw 285 street mutts arrested. By February 1968, the city was arresting 500 dogs a month and wondering where to jail the rest. One city official suggested giving each prisoner in the county jail one as a pet, but that official does not wish to receive credit for the suggestion.

While City Hall was wrestling with such monumental problems, Mobile was undergoing all sorts of changes and improvements. The International Trade Center was opened in November, 1966. The U.S.S. Alabama arrived in Mobile after a spirited state-wide campaign in which the school children of Alabama helped raise the necessary funds. Mobile got its first real skyscraper when the thirty-three-story First National Bank Building was erected.

Then the new Municipal Auditorium was completed which brought to Mobile the greatest entertainment in the world, from ice shows to track meets.

The revolution in civic improvements seems to get more ambitious with each turn of the calendar page. A Spanish Plaza has just been completed, a new tunnel is about to be drilled, an International Airport may be in the making; then a new library, perhaps later, a Southern Disneyland, an Eiffel tower, an . . . while other Mobilians are wondering when the Bankhead Tunnel will be freed, who keeps painting the cannon, what causes the Kali Oka Mystery lights, who killed Jim Waldrup, what will ever happen to the *Tecumseh* . . . ?